PRIMER
FOR
REVOLT

*The Communist Takeover
in Viet-Nam*

TRUONG CHINH

PRIMER
FOR
REVOLT

THE COMMUNIST TAKEOVER IN VIET-NAM

A Facsimile Edition of
THE AUGUST REVOLUTION
and
THE RESISTANCE WILL WIN

by Trường-Chinh

Trư ớ'ng - Chinh

With an Introduction and Notes by

Bernard B. Fall

FREDERICK A. PRAEGER, *Publisher*
New York • London

FREDERICK A. PRAEGER, PUBLISHER
64 UNIVERSITY PLACE, NEW YORK 3, N.Y., U.S.A.
49 GREAT ORMOND STREET, LONDON W.C. 1, ENGLAND

Published in the United States of America in 1963
by Frederick A. Praeger, Inc., Publisher

This book is Number 133 in the series of
Praeger Publications in Russian History and World Communism.

Printed in the United States of America

CONTENTS

TRUONG CHINH: *Portrait of a Party Thinker*

By Bernard B. Fall

In every Communist regime, there is a man who likes to think of himself as a manipulator rather than an "operator" —as the *deus ex machina* of the system within which he lives.

This is almost always a taxing role, and within the Communist system, many a would-be *éminence grise* or Party Machiavelli has paid with his life for an error of judgment that made his superiors consider him dangerous or expendable. Within the remarkably stable leadership of Communist North Viet-Nam (officially, the Democratic Republic of Viet-Nam, or D.R.V.N.), one man has occupied this challenging post for nearly thirty years almost without interruption. His name is Dang Xuan Khu, but he is better known under the pseudonym of "Truong Chinh."

The choice of that pseudonym—it is the literal Vietnamese translation of the Chinese expression meaning the "Long March"—is in itself revelatory of the man's character and leanings. In a country that is traditionally anti-Chinese, and in a Communist state that maintains a precarious balance between Moscow and Peking, Truong Chinh stands at a political extreme in favoring full cooperation with Peking. But that is not his only peculiarity. Among his colleagues, he is one of the few who do not come from the middle class of northern Central Viet-Nam and who do not have any foreign political experience. He is also the only

North Vietnamese Communist thus far to have produced anything approaching a truly articulate statement of the aims of the Vietnamese Communist revolution.

Neither Ho Chi Minh nor General Vo Nguyên Giap—both far better known than Truong Chinh both inside the Vietnamese movement and abroad—has written anything that can be considered a contribution to historical knowledge about the movement. Both deal in Party-line platitudes which are eagerly scrutinized in the United States today more because of the woeful lack of hard information about Vietnamese Communist operations than because of the intrinsic value of the writings.

This is not true of the writings of Truong Chinh, whose two major works appear on the following pages. Even in the far from perfect English translation prepared in Hanoi from the Vietnamese original, his style has a refreshing directness rarely achieved by Communist writers. Truong Chinh is free of the verbosity of a Mao Tse-tung and the tendency toward overphilosophizing that is the hallmark of the Western-trained Communist. His books are simple statements of the facts as he saw them in 1945–47 and embody simple recommendations for bolstering the position of the Viet-Minh revolutionaries in their fight against the French.

This is a Communist who coldly tells his followers, as they are about to enter a war against a formidable Western force, that they "lack generally a sense of organization. Our work is still routine, non-scientific and without perspective." He warns his own side against the advocates of military solutions who "tend to believe that everything can be settled by armed force" and thus fail to "apply political mobilization." The latter criticism, whose validity is as great in counterinsurgency operations as in insurgency itself, is being understood only very reluctantly on our side of the fence; there is much evidence that, in South Viet-Nam and elsewhere, our side tends to rely on military solutions instead of political reforms it feels incapable of imposing upon the regimes we support.

But what is perhaps most important about Truong Chinh's work is that it has remained *timeless*. The conclusions the author draws, based simply upon his own readings and upon what he observed during his relatively brief stay in China, are as valid in 1963 as they were in 1947. Thus, in 1959, when General Giap wrote *People's War, People's Army,* he was in fact assiduously borrowing from Truong Chinh's *The Resistance Will Win.* Giap admits this in his own book (p. 102), where he hails Truong Chinh's little opus as "an important contribution to the thorough understanding of the Resistance War line." It was Truong Chinh, rather than Mao, that Giap read as he prepared his first offensive against the French, in 1950–51; and it was in all likelihood a misreading of Truong Chinh that led Giap into the disastrous three-pronged offensive of 1951 against Marshal de Lattre de Tassigny that cost the People's Army two divisions and set the Viet-Minh timetable back a full year. There is now strong evidence that Truong Chinh was an important member of the quadrumvirate (including also Ho Chi Minh, Pham Van Dong, and Giap) that led the struggle against the French until 1954, although official North Vietnamese propaganda tends to credit General Giap with all the military achievements of the war. But it is in keeping with Truong Chinh's make-up as an *éminence grise* that he has never claimed credit for his role as a revolutionary-warfare strategist. Yet, anyone who, as early as 1947, had the good sense to remind his colleagues that *"Guerrilla warfare must be the tactic of the people as a whole, not of the army alone"*[1] surely deserves a niche among the more sophisticated

[1] Cf. p. 116.

thinkers on the art. One could wish that this phrase could be engraved in bold letters above every American installation where revolutionary warfare is being planned or taught.

As will be seen later, Truong Chinh went far beyond the lip service to "self-criticism" usual among Communist thinkers when they examine problems in their own backyard. *The August Revolution* deserves careful study not only by Western political experts, but also by the politicians of underdeveloped countries, because it provides a perfect blueprint for a Communist *coup d'état:* creation of a united front with the non-Communist nationalists, outflanking of the nationalist elements through better organization and greater maneuverability, and a healthy dose of opportunism. It enabled the Vietnamese Communists and the Viet-Minh front to get hold of the bulk of the Japanese garrisons' weapons and to capture Hanoi and Saigon before the old-style Vietnamese nationalists and their Chinese protectors (or, for that matter, the British occupation forces in South Viet-Nam or the American liaison teams in the North) had time even to set foot on Vietnamese soil. And exactly as the Communists had intended all along, they were now in a position, "as the people's power, to welcome the Allied forces."[2] And thus the Allies as well as the Vietnamese nationalists had lost the first round of the Indochina War eighteen months before the first shot was fired. Truong Chinh may not have devised the whole grand strategy of that takeover himself, but he most certainly was one of the central characters in the play, and he alone of all the participants took the time to record the events as he saw them, or as he wanted his public to believe he saw them. The notes I have added to his text will attempt to straighten out the historical record where Truong Chinh has seen fit to bend it somewhat to suit his particular ideology.

[2] Cf. p. 14.

As in the case of all of Viet-Nam's Communist leaders, very little verifiable information is available on Truong Chinh personally. He was born on February 15, 1909, in Hanh Thien, a small textile town in the southern Red River Delta province of Nam-Dinh. His parents were Dang Xuan Bien and Nguyên Thi Tu. His father, a local schoolteacher, wanted his oldest son to follow in his footsteps. Thus, Truong Chinh was reared to respect scholarship and intellectual achievement. He was also reared in the spirit of resistance against the foreign occupier of his country. In North Viet-Nam, for centuries the shield against Chinese invasions and also the last Vietnamese territory to fall under French control, that spirit was very much alive; and Truong Chinh, like Ho and Giap, became an ardent revolutionary in his early teens, while still boarding at the Nam-Dinh high school. In 1928, he joined the Revolutionary Youth League (Thanh-Nien Cach-Menh Dong Chi Hoi) created by Ho Chi Minh in South China in 1925, and participated in the general student strikes in the spring of that year.

In Nam-Dinh, the strike grew in extent and violence, and Truong Chinh was among the many students who were first arrested and then expelled from school by the colonial authorities; and thus, he followed the same pattern as his later associates Ho, Dong, and Giap, all of whom had begun their revolutionary careers as high-school "agitators."

Truong Chinh, barred from Nam-Dinh, transferred to the renowned Lycée Albert Sarraut in Hanoi,[3] where he received his French baccalaureate degree. He then enrolled in the School of Higher Commercial Studies and, again like his

[3] When this writer was in Hanoi, in July, 1962, the Lycée Albert Sarraut, named after one of France's colonial governors, still operated in the North Vietnamese capital under its old name and directly opposite the D.R.V.N. Presidential palace. Its original name is retained apparently for the same reason that the Indians keep the statues of their former British viceroys—sentiment.

friend and associate of later years, Giap, Truong Chinh became a private teacher in order to eke out a living while continuing his studies. But he also had become involved in politics and had joined the Indochinese Communist Party (ICP), created by Ho Chi Minh in January, 1930. Truong Chinh also became co-editor of *Bua-Liem (Sickle and Hammer),* one of Viet-Nam's earliest Communist publications. Therefore, when the Communists decided to take charge of a hopeless peasant rebellion in Nghé-An Province in the summer of 1930, he was a prime target of the French police. Arrested in Hanoi on November 2, 1930, he was held without trial until September 28, 1931. On that date, the French Criminal Court of Hanoi sentenced him to twelve years of penal servitude for "conspiring against the security of the state."

The ensuing years were hard on the young Communist teacher; he was transferred from the *maison centrale* in Hanoi to the ill-famed Son-La forced-labor camp, in the mosquito-infested Thai tribal area, where hundreds of other ICP members and anti-French nationalists were carving roads out of the jungle. Like political prisons and concentration camps elsewhere in the world, Son-La had become a "Communist Party university," where the hard-core Communists perfected the ideological indoctrination of the Party newcomers and converted the non-Communist prisoners to the righteousness of their cause—a process that goes on to this day. By the time Truong Chinh was paroled, on September 29, 1936, after a Popular Front regime had come to power in France, he had acquired a reputation as a capable organizer and one of the best theoreticians in the ICP.

And the ICP badly needed new blood. Its first Secretary-General, Tran Phu, had been arrested in Saigon in March, 1931, and had died in prison on September 5 of that year. Ho Chi Minh had been arrested by the British in Hong

Kong on June 5 and, released later that year, had to go underground in Shanghai. In fact, the ICP was so disorganized that the Thai Communist Party had to come to its rescue, and ICP cells among Vietnamese settlers there and in Laos had to provide cadres for their parent organization in Viet-Nam. In addition, the ICP got embroiled in a typically Communist ideological fight with the Trotskyites in its midst. Its second Secretary-General, Lê Hong Phong, was likewise unable to hold the field inside Viet-Nam, in the face of the superbly organized political section of the French Sûreté— beyond doubt one of the best secret police organizations outside the Soviet orbit. He established his temporary headquarters in the nearby Portuguese colony of Macao in the spring of 1933, while inside Viet-Nam, the unified Central Committee was abolished altogether in June, 1934, because it was no longer possible to coordinate operations throughout the country. It was replaced by two regional committees: one for the North and Laos, another for southern Central Viet-Nam, South Viet-Nam, and Cambodia. The ICP inside Viet-Nam thus drifted leaderless until liberalization measures taken by the French left-wing government opened prison doors throughout the Indochinese peninsula. The general amnesty of 1936 brought the emergence of a new category of Vietnamese Communists—not the "parlor pinks" who argued Marx in Paris' Latin Quarter, but a group of prison-hardened Party fanatics who had scores to settle and who harbored no illusions about peaceful co-existence with the colonial administration.

But Lê Hong Phong, who had attended the Seventh Comintern Congress, in Moscow in July, 1935, now faced the unpopular task of having to adjust the ICP's policies to the new "Dimitrov Line" of cooperation with the colonial powers in the face of the mounting danger presented in

Europe and Asia by the fascist powers. Truong Chinh adhered to the new line without a murmur. Operating again
in Hanoi, he became the co-editor of and contributor to
three newspapers of the Democratic United Front, the "legal
struggle" organization with which the hard-core ICP had
surrounded itself. His incisive articles on world affairs and
on agrarian problems brought him to the attention of the
ICP leadership, and he came into contact with many of his
later colleagues, such as Pham Van Dong and Giap. With
the latter, he soon developed a close friendship that apparently survived subsequent differences in viewpoint.

With the coming of World War II, and the U.S.S.R.'s
cynical pact with Nazi Germany, came the end of the honey-
moon between the colonial administration and the ICP.
After the outbreak of the war, on September 3, 1939, the
French Communist Party was banned in France when its
leaders exhorted their followers to refuse to serve in the
army against the Nazis, and then fled to sit out the war in
Moscow; and on September 28, 1939, the ban was extended
to the Party in Indochina as well.

In the ensuing round-up of ICP adherents, more than two
hundred were arrested, among them, Truong Chinh. Ar-
raigned before the French *juge d'instruction* of Hanoi on
October 4 for possession of "illegal publications," he managed to convince the judge of his innocence, and the charges
against him were dismissed. Soon after, he disappeared from
view. According to American sources, he went to the Red
Chinese base at Yenan: French sources assert that he went
only as far as Yünnan or Kwang-si, bordering on North
Viet-Nam, which had provided asylum for many Vietnamese
refugee groups in the past. The latter is more likely, as
Truong Chinh is reported to have participated on October
6, 1940, at the seventh meeting of the Tong-Bô (Central

Committee), held in Bac-Ninh, twenty-five miles north of Hanoi.[4]

But even before that event, the ICP had again been showing signs of ideological confusion. Like most other Communist parties, it had for years been geared toward an antifascist struggle, with the clear understanding that its anti-colonial struggle at home would have to take second priority. Now, because of Russia's good relations with Germany, the struggle against France had to be intensified, but on the other hand, the psychological appeal of the anti-Axis issue could not be entirely forfeited. The communiqué issued on November 13, 1939, at the conclusion of the sixth meeting of the Tong-Bô of the ICP, thus stressed that

> . . . the struggle against the policy of massacres and rob-bery of the French imperialists has become a matter of life and death for the peoples of Indochina, so as to abol-ish its yoke while continuing to struggle against the ag-gressive designs of Japanese fascism. . . .

During this period also, Party leadership once more changed hands: Lê Hong Phong was taken prisoner by the ubiquitous Sûreté late in 1939, along with such stalwarts as Ha Huy Tap and Lê Duan, who became Party Secretary-General in 1960. Lê Hong Phong died under the guillotine late in 1940.[5] His successor, Nguyên Van Cu, had hardly better luck: He was arrested shortly after the Bac-Ninh meet-

[4] *Trente ans du Parti de la classe ouvrière vietnamienne* (Hanoi: Foreign Languages Publishing House, 1960), p. 72.

[5] Available sources show a certain conflict of dates. The authori-tative French writer Philippe Devillers, in his *Histoire du Viet-Nam de 1940 à 1952* (Paris: Editions du Seuil, 1952), states that Lê Hong Phong was arrested in June, 1939 (p. 72). *Trente ans . . .* states that he was arrested just when the Japanese troops entered Viet-Nam, i.e., in September–October, 1940. In 1950, the Viet-Minh named their first major offensive against the French after him.

ing and also executed, along with Ha Huy Tap, Mme.
Nguyên Thi Minh-Khai, and other members of the Tong-
Bô. This time, the ICP simply gave up the game. All its key
members received orders to retreat into China for the time
being. Truong Chinh, as one of the few surviving members
of the old Party organization inside Indochina, became a
member of the reconstituted Provisional Central Committee
that operated with the ICP remnants in South China until
Ho Chi Minh, along with a Red Chinese guerrilla-training
mission under Yeh Chien-ying (now a Chinese field marshal), arrived late in 1940 and took the movement in hand
again.

Ho Chi Minh was impressed with the tough, smooth-
browed organizer who, far from trying to save face for all
concerned, bluntly told his colleagues where they (and he)
had erred. At the key eighth meeting of the Tong-Bô, between May 10 and 19, 1941, in the Pac-Bo grottoes in Cao-
Bang Province,[6] Truong Chinh emerged as the ICP's new
Secretary-General. In less than five years, he had reached
the pinnacle of his Party's hierarchy.

Much has been made of Truong Chinh's Red Chinese
associations and alleged lengthy stay in the Red Chinese
Yenan stronghold. One semi-official British source even
went so far as to assert that Truong Chinh had served in
the Red Chinese 8th Route Army. But as one delves into
Truong Chinh's life, it becomes apparent that his pro-
Chinese inclinations are based on factors other than a long
personal association with Chinese Communism. In fact,
most other present-day North Vietnamese leaders had longer

[6] Some sources (including my own earlier writings) tend to place
this conference in Tsing-hsi Province, China (about fifty miles east
of Cao-Bang). For psychological purposes, however, the Communist Vietnamese mythology now asserts that this meeting took
place on Vietnamese soil.

or more intimate association with the Chinese Reds than did Truong Chinh; for, if he went to Yenan at all, it must have been *after* he had been appointed Secretary-General of the ICP and while Ho Chi Minh was in a Chinese Nationalist prison in Kwang-si.[7] In other words, it would have meant that he had left the ICP virtually leaderless in the midst of a major crisis. There is not the slightest doubt that Truong Chinh early developed a preference for the blunt tactics of the Red Chinese, but there is no proof that he ever spent any time at Yenan or in the Chinese 8th Route Army.

In any case, Truong Chinh was in the Vietnamese frontier area on February 25, 1943, when the ICP—which had now become the core of a more broadly based front organization known as the Viet-Minh—proclaimed a "minimum program" embodying the overthrow of both the "Japanese and French fascists" in Indochina, and independence and democracy for the three countries of the peninsula. Truong Chinh was also there when the first Viet-Minh guerrilla units were set up by his friend Giap in October, 1944, but what is probably his finest hour came in the summer of 1945, when he engineered the Vietnamese Communist takeover of the anti-French revolution in Viet-Nam. That operation, described with great candor in the first book of this volume, *The August Revolution,* ranks with the Communist takeover of Czechoslovakia in smoothness and cold-blooded efficiency. It fooled not only the Chinese Nationalist forces that entered North Viet-Nam in September, 1945, but also the various American missions operating in the area, which

[7] Ho Chi Minh was imprisoned by warlord Chiang Fa-k'wei from August 28, 1942, to September 16, 1943, in order to persuade him to accept the creation of a Vietnamese "government in exile" dominated by Kuomintang elements. He agreed in order to gain his freedom but soon thereafter ousted the Kuomintang elements. Cf. Bernard B. Fall, *The Two Viet-Nams* (New York: Frederick A. Praeger, 1963).

were led to believe that Ho Chi Minh's regime consisted of old-fashioned nationalists and agrarian reformers.[8]

With the occupation of Hanoi by the Viet-Minh in August, 1945, and the proclamation of the Democratic Republic of Viet-Nam on September 2, Truong Chinh's role as Party leader and intimate friend of Vo Nguyên Giap brought him to the center of the decision-making process within the D.R.V.N. In all probability, it also brought him for the first time into disagreement with Ho Chi Minh, who wanted to negotiate a permanent settlement with France, while Giap publicly advocated what was called the "Brest-Litovsk Doctrine," i.e., a temporary settlement with France until the Viet-Minh was ready for the next round. Appraising the situation with cold realism, Ho calculated that outside Communist aid was far away and that survival of his regime depended on the good will of the Chinese Nationalist warlords and American missions present in Hanoi; Ho decided simply to abolish the ICP altogether.

In the course of a special congress of the Party Central Committee, the ICP was dissolved, on November 10, 1945, "in order not to harm national unity." Actually, of course, the Party never ceased to exist; its functions were taken over by an "Association of Marxist Studies" whose chairman was Truong Chinh. That "Association" replaced the official Party machinery until the Viet-Minh was certain that no further propaganda advantage could be won by concealing the Communist character of the regime. In February, 1951, a congress was held in the Viet-Minh redoubt of Thai-Nguyên, in the course of which it was decided to abolish the Viet-Minh front organization. On March 4, 1951, the new Vietnamese Communist Party, shorn of its Cam-

[8] For an example of that viewpoint, see Ellen J. Hammer, *The Emergence of Viet-Nam* (New York: Institute of Pacific Relations, 1947).

bodian and Laotian appendages,[9] was born under the name Viet-Nam Dang Lao-Dong, or Vietnamese Labor Party. Truong Chinh, as before, was its Secretary-General.

But Truong Chinh came into his own as a Party philosopher during the hectic 1945–46 period, while the Ho Chi Minh regime was going through the birthpangs of its organization in the face of the Chinese Nationalist occupation—which ceased finally in February, 1946—and French hostility. *The August Revolution,* published first in serialized form in the newspaper *Su-That (The Truth),* will stand as a model of clarity in explaining both the positive and negative factors affecting the position of the Viet-Minh during that crucial period. Truong Chinh's second work, *The Resistance Will Win,* written when the Viet-Minh struggle against France was at its lowest ebb, is truly admirable in its level-headed appraisal of the strengths and weaknesses not only of the French position but also of the Viet-Minh's. Many of Truong Chinh's warnings in 1947 to his associates "who have a tendency only to rely on military action," and who "tend to believe that everything can be settled by armed force," could have been addressed in 1963 by Western advisers to their own associates in South Viet-Nam.

It is this depth of long-range thinking that differentiates Truong Chinh from his colleagues, who are by and large "operators" and whose writings reveal that they are not deeply concerned with the ideological details of properly interpreting Marxism-Leninism. This perhaps explains why Truong Chinh espoused the Red Chinese view of Communism, and why, after the Geneva cease-fire of 1954, he became the most ardent advocate in North Viet-Nam of

[9] The ICP, although Vietnamese-dominated, included Laotian and Cambodian elements. The new Party, though ostensibly Vietnamese, of course retained operational control of the still weak "Free Khmer" and Pathet-Lao movements.

following the Chinese in their abrupt collectivization of agriculture. The Lao-Dong Party played a key role in implementing the Viet-Minh land reform through a system of trials and summary executions of landlords in open imitation of the methods applied in neighboring China. According to one South Vietnamese source, Truong Chinh's own father was tried as a "reactionary" before the People's Court of Hanh-Thien village, in Bui-Chu Province, in 1955.[10] While the source is obviously biased and the incident perhaps invented, it is significant that Truong Chinh is believed to be the kind of person capable of allowing his own father to be tried on such a charge.

Little wonder, then, that Truong Chinh was the ideal scapegoat when the brutal land-collectivization policy backfired in the fall of 1956. During the tenth enlarged session of the Central Committee, held late in October, Truong Chinh "confessed" that he had committed "major errors" in his function as head of the Central Land Reform Committee and was dismissed from his post as Secretary-General of the Party. For the first time since the inception of the Vietnamese Communist movement, Ho took this post for himself, concurrently with that of Party President, which he had held since 1930. Two other members of the Central Committee who had been associated with Truong Chinh— Ho Viet Thang and Lê Van Luong—were also dismissed from their posts. But those last-minute changes and the ensuing "rectification-of-errors" campaign could not head off the explosion of peasant furor that followed. On November 4, 1956 (a date overshadowed by events occurring at Suez and Budapest), the peasants of Ho's own native province of Nghé-An rebelled against the D.R.V.N. Administration and had to be put down with regular troops.

[10] *Ngon-Luan* (Saigon), July 27, 1955.

But Truong Chinh's demotion—like the dissolution of the ICP in 1945—was a move dictated by local tactics rather than an indication of permanent disgrace. This was evident since Truong Chinh retained his membership in the Party Secretariat and the Political Bureau, whereas his lower-ranking associates were demoted from their Party functions and fired from their high positions in the land-reform and agricultural bureaus.[11] It is possible that Truong Chinh was dealt with leniently because of fear that his total disgrace would have been resented by Peking as an implicit disavowal of its policies; but it is also likely that the D.R.V.N. leadership simply recognized that it was collectively responsible for the land-reform blunders and that Truong Chinh's temporary eclipse would be a cheap price to pay to assuage the irate peasantry.

The fact remains that, far from disappearing from public view, Truong Chinh continued to appear at important public functions; and, on April 29, 1958, a terse announcement from Hanoi brought the news that he had been named a Vice-Premier along with Giap and two other senior officials. In December of that year, he was appointed to the Presidency of North Viet-Nam's Scientific Research Council. However, his total rehabilitation did not come until 1960, when he presented himself as a candidate for the legislature of the D.R.V.N. in the elections held on May 8—the sixth anniversary of the battle of Dien Bien Phu. Truong Chinh was re-elected with a greater plurality of votes than the incumbent Secretary-General of the Party, Lê Duan, to whom Ho had relinquished the post. On July 15, he was appointed to the important post of Chairman of the Standing Committee of the National Assembly, i.e., the small group of

[11] J. H. Brimmell, *Communism in South East Asia: A Political Analysis* (London and New York: Oxford University Press, 1959), p. 301.

legislators that, like the Presidium of the Supreme Soviet, has legislative powers in the absence of the regular parliament.

In the past, Truong Chinh has often been mentioned as a potential successor to Ho Chi Minh, or as a contender for power with Giap or Pham Van Dong. There is little evidence to support this conjecture. Beyond a doubt, within the Communist orbit, Truong Chinh is the most widely known Vietnamese after Ho and Giap—but this does not assure him of popularity at home. In his relentless pursuit of a hard Party line, in bluntly pointing out the mistakes of his associates over the past twenty years, in accepting responsibility for the earlier failures of the land reform, and, finally, in allowing himself to be marked as the "man of Peking" in a country where distrust of China is part of the national heritage—Truong Chinh has probably forfeited his chances of becoming a popular leader.

But as the following pages show, Truong Chinh fully deserves to be included among the few contemporary Communists who have made a far-reaching contribution to the revolutionary theory of their own movement.

B. B. F.

Howard University
Washington, D.C.
April 1, 1963

Note to Readers of This Facsimile Edition

In the original volumes, Truong Chinh's footnotes were designated by asterisks (*), as they appear here. The footnotes added by Bernard B. Fall are designated by numbers.

TRUONG CHINH

THE
AUGUST REVOLUTION

(Second Edition)

[FACSIMILE EDITION]

HANOI
FOREIGN LANGUAGES PUBLISHING HOUSE
1 9 6 2

CONTENTS

PUBLISHERS' NOTE

Truong Chinh, member of the Political Bureau of the Central Committee of the Viet Nam Workers' Party, Chairman of the National Assembly of the Democratic Republic of Viet Nam, wrote the "August Revolution" in 1946, on the occasion of the first anniversary of this momentous event, the cornerstone in our history.

Since then, great changes have taken place in our country. Dien Bien Phu and the Geneva Agreements have brought the long war of resistance to a victorious end. Under the leadership of the Viet Nam Workers' Party and President Ho Chi Minh, our people are now waging a peaceful struggle to unite their country and build up socialism step by step in the completely liberated zone of North Viet Nam.

We deem it right to say that although this book was written in 1946, it still has high interest, not only because of the importance of the events it deals with, but also because of the personality of the writer who, in his capacity as General Secretary of the Indochinese Communist Party, played a prominent role in the August Revolution in 1945.

PREFACE

to the 1946 Vietnamese edition

Dear readers,

This little book is a collection of articles published in the newspaper " Su That" (The Truth) on the occasion of the first anniversary of the August Revolution. The articles have been revised, and filled out. Some passages have been re-written.

Our only aim is to relate the history of the heroic struggle of our people, to submit it to an impartial criticism, to determine the character and the significance of the August Revolution, to outline its development for the future and, lastly, to reveal to our compatriots the immediate main tasks in view for the realisation of national independence, freedom and happiness.

At the present time, there are people who have not lost a drop of sweat for the revolution, or who have acted and are acting as traitors, who try to deny the importance of the August Revolution. They pretend that our people[12] did not struggle so hard and that they got possession of power by " chance ". Against this point of view which stems from obvious bad faith, we have only to remember here the phases of our people's struggle in the " Great

---

[12] Truong Chinh refers to the Vietnamese nationalists who refused to co-operate with the Viet-Minh movement and who asserted that Viet-Minh military operations against the Japanese had been of little importance.

National Salvation Movement against the Japanese fascists" as well as in the August General Insurrection : we particularly stress the leading role and organising work of the Indochinese Communist Party and the Viet Minh Front as well as their skilful agitation tactics in the preparatory period of the insurrection.

Besides, to check the policy of the French colonialists — a policy of aggression and of successive encroachments in the military field, and of division and deception in the political field — we outline the details of this single path for the salvation and building of the country at this stage, the path of union and of struggle mapped out for our people by President Ho Chi Minh.

The August General Insurrection, like the Great National Salvation Movement against the Japanese fascists, is a struggle varied in forms and rich in content. This book would not dare pretend to contain the full story of its manifold experiences. We hope that the fighters in our national liberation movement will draw further experiences from it in order to complete this book.

In any case, the following pages will be of some use if they succeed in strengthening the reader's faith in the success of the task of national liberation, and help him to understand better his civic duties : to fully understand the policy advocated by the communists in our country for the present period and the great effectiveness of certain Marxist-Leninist methods of mobilizing the masses, adapted to the situation in Indo-China.

The August Revolution is only one of the first victories of the national liberation movement. We shall have to fight harder battles to safeguard our national sovereignty and territorial integrity, to consolidate our democratic republican regime and to achieve our total independence.

The struggle for national liberation is extremely hard, but it will surely achieve complete victory. We firmly believe this and now invite the reader to review with us our recent heroic struggle so as to prepare ourselves for future struggles.

TRUONG CHINH
Hanoi, September 20, 1946

CHAPTER I

A GLORIOUS PAGE IN OUR HISTORY

The high tide of the anti-Japanese movement

On March 9, 1945, in Indo-China, the Japanese fascists swept the French colonialists out of the political arena. In less than twenty-four hours, in all the main towns, the French colonialists laid down their arms and surrendered to the Japanese. Some French units scuttled to the frontier. At Cao Bang and Bac Can, others made an attempt to co-operate with the *Liberation Army* in the fight against the Japanese fascists. At Bac Can, a "Franco-Vietnamese resistance committee against the Japanese fascists" was organized. But after a time, the French left us and fled to China. * It can be said that the French troops in Indo-China did not resist the Japanese, and that the Resistance was the work of our own people only.[13]

---

* *Although Major Reul at Cao Bang and Lieutenant Pontiche at Bac Can ordered their troops to co-operate with the Liberation Army, it was to avoid being disarmed by our forces rather than to carry on the struggle against the Japanese fascists. They fled before waging even a single battle on our side.*

[13] That is inaccurate. The French, though surprised, fought on in the North Vietnamese highlands and Laos for almost three months. The French garrisons at Dong-Dang and Lang-Son stood their ground to the last. More than 250 officers and 4,000 men fell in the course of these operations.

On the very night of March 9, the Bureau of the Central Standing Committee of the Indochinese Communist Party, at a meeting held at Tu Son (Bac Ninh province), about 30 km. from Hanoi, decided to give a strong boost to the " Great National Salvation Movement against the Japanese Fascists".

The next day, in the Hoang Hoa Tham resistance zone (High and Middle Regions of North Viet Nam), the guerillas took the isolated posts by storm, disarmed a number of French soldiers and Bao An * units to pre_ vent their arms from falling into the hands of the Japanese; they attacked the Japanese troops moving along the roads of Tuyen Quang, Thai Nguyen, Bac Can and Cao Bang provinces, harassed them even in the chief town of Bac Can province, and launched sudden attacks against their base at Cho Chu, etc. In North and Central Viet Nam, thousands of paddy stores set up by the Japanese were stormed by the people and their paddy stocks distributed to the poor. In this way the famine was relieved by revolutionary means. In Bac Giang, Thai Nguyen, Bac Can and other provinces, the peasants rose up, seized and distributed land held by the Japanese and French.

Most of the attacks against the paddy stores became armed parades and demonstrations. Armed Viet Minh militants harangued the masses at cross-roads and in market-places to win them over to the national cause. The illusion that the Japanese fascists could be useful to us, that they had come to free us, etc. was vigorously combated by the masses and revolutionary

---

* Bao An: troops ensuring the puppet government's security.

ranks. In main towns, *picked units* of the Viet Minh
Front, operating under the noses of the Japanese
troops, killed the dangerous traitors and the predatory
Japanese officers, sowing confusion in the ranks of
the Japanese fascists and their lackeys. Everywhere,
self-defence units or guerilla teams developed quickly.
Everyone feverishly sought to get any kind of weapon so as to be ready to hurl himself at the enemy at
the first opportunity. *Peoples' Committees* were founded
in the regions controlled by the guerillas. In other
zones, *Liberation Committees* sprang up like mushrooms
and began on the one hand to lead the masses in the
preparations for the general insurrection and on the
other hand, to train them to exercise power.

The Revolution was gaining incredible strength.
The pre-insurrectionary atmosphere prevailed everywhere, arousing the enthusiasm of the members of
organisations for national salvation and winning over
even the wavering elements.

In April, the Revolutionary Military Conference
of North Viet Nam held at Bac Giang, drew up the
general insurrection preparatory plan and formed the
High Command of the *North Viet Nam Liberation
Army*.

In June, by decision of the conference of cadres
from the six provinces of Cao Bang, Lang Son, Ha
Giang, Bac Can, Tuyen Quang and Thai Nguyen,
convened by the Viet Minh General Committee, the
free zone was officially founded including the territory of these six provinces and unifying the various
regions placed under the control of the revolutionary

power. The *New Viet Nam* came into being. The people's committees adopted energetic measures to suppress the fascist militarists' forms of oppression and exploitation, actively break the colonialist chains and improve the people's living conditions. A part of North Viet Nam was effectively controlled by the revolutionary power, a situation which provided the August General Insurrection with extremely favourable preliminary conditions.

From June on, the Allied Air Forces launched massive attacks against Japan.

In July, at the Potsdam Conference, the Soviet Union decided to participate in the war against Japan. The Viet Minh General Committee, headed by comrade Ho Chi Minh, sped up the convening of the National Congress. But, because of difficulties of communication, the Congress could not be held until August, in the liberated zone only, and at the very moment of the Japanese capitulation.

The August Insurrection

On August 9, the Soviet Red Army launched a powerful attack on Manchuria, and within six days, the crack Japanese Kwantung Army was entirely routed.

This decisive victory of the Soviet Army decided the fate of the Japanese fascists ; the Soviet Union had liberated the peoples subjected to Japanese oppression.[14]

The situation of Japan became hopeless and it was then that the Communist Party, which was at the

---

[14] Note the suppression, as early as 1946, of the preponderant American contribution to the defeat of Japan and the emphasis on Russia's victories in her six-day war against Japan.

time holding its National Congress, took a decision to launch the general insurrection and to found the democratic republican regime in Viet Nam. The Viet Minh General Committee approved these decisions and the *Insurrection Committee* was immediately set up. At the news of the imminent unconditional surrender of Japan, this Committee gave the order on the night of August 13, for the launching of the general insurrection.

In the morning of August 16, the *People's Congress* was held at Tan Trao village, Tuyen Quang province, in the *free zone*. More than 60 delegates from big and small national minorities and of all political convictions in our country, gathering in an atmosphere of friendship and great enthusiasm, approved the Viet Minh General Committee's order for general insurrection, decided upon the domestic and foreign policies of the revolutionary power and appointed the *Liberation National Committee of Viet Nam*, i. e. the Provisional Government of the *Democratic Republic of Viet Nam*.

After many years of perilous peregrinations and of clandestine activities, comrade Ho Chi Minh appeared for the first time before the people's delegates.

Because the people's Congress opened immediately after the general insurrection order had been launched, it had to hold a "lightning" session allow-[15] ing the delegates to return quickly to their local regions and, together with the local militants to lead the decisive struggle. (In fact, as early as August 10, some delegates bound for the Congress received the order to turn back).

---

[15] The non-Communist members of the Viet-Minh were to charge later that the "lightning" session enabled the Communists to take over the liberation movement from within.

During the historic Congress, the Indochinese Communist Party advocated an extremely clear policy : to lead the masses in insurrection in order to disarm the Japanese before the arrival of the Allied forces in Indo-China; to wrest power from the Japanese and their puppet stooges and finally, as the people's power, to welcome the Allied forces coming to disarm the Japanese troops stationed in Indo-China.[16]

In numerous localities, taking advantage of the extreme confusion of the Japanese forces, who were conscious of their imminent defeat, the Viet Minh militants, implementing the instructions given by the Communist Party in March, took the initiative to lead the people to rise up and seize power even before receiving the general insurrection order : as for example the insurrection at Ha Tinh on August 11, at Quang Ngai on August 13, and the taking of several Japanese posts in the vicinity of the *free zone* on August 14 and 15. On August 16, the news of the Japanese surrender began to spread rapidly. In all provinces, huge public meetings accompanied by armed demonstrations were held in the public thoroughfares. A great number of factories and public offices ceased work. The gold starred red flag was seen waving everywhere. Many armed demonstrations were transformed into sudden attacks on Japanese posts. On August 17 and 18, hundreds of thousands of people demonstrated in Hanoi. A general political strike began. The Viet Minh delegates called on the masses to seize power. On August 19, the entire capital rose up. The Bao An troops and police detachments tended towards the Revolutionary forces. The insurrectional forces headed

---

[16] This paragraph is a clear and explicit summing-up of Communist Vietnamese strategy at that time. It succeeded fully.

by their vanguard shock detachments of youths and workers and led by the Viet Minh cadres, took by storm the hotel where the Imperial Delegate [17] had been residing. The latter, however, had fled with his lackeys. The Viet Minh League proclaimed the foundation of the provisional revolutionary power. Faced with the irresistible growth of the revolutionary movement of the entire nation and people, united as one, Bao Dai abdicated. The Tran Trong Kim puppet government surrendered. The Viet Minh General Committee sent their delegates to Hue to receive the King's abdication.

The birth of the Democratic Republic of Viet Nam

A few days later, almost all members of the *Viet Nam Liberation National Committee* met in Hanoi. In conformity with the new situation, the Committee was reformed to include some non-party personalities and to constitute a provisional unified national government presided over by Ho Chi Minh. On August 29, 1945, a detachment of the *Liberation Army* from the resistance zone, entered Hanoi, hailed by the thunderous ovation of an enthusiastic crowd. On September 2, President Ho Chi Minh appeared before the people in Hanoi's Ba Dinh square where nearly 500,000 people gathered in a huge meeting to hear the first President of new Viet Nam read the *Proclamation of Independence* of the Democratic Republic of Viet Nam to the Vietnamese people and to the world.

On August 23, in Saigon-Cholon, a million of our compatriots demonstrated in the streets. The South Viet Nam Administrative Committee was founded.

---

[17] The word "hotel" is used here in its French secondary sense, i.e., official residence. The imperial delegate (*kham-sai*, or viceroy) was Phan Ké Toai. An appointee of Bao-Dai, he later changed his views, switched over to the Viet-Minh, and in 1955 became Minister of the Interior of the D.R.V.N. He lost the post in May, 1963.

The vanguard youth and militia seized power in the provinces and united to form the revolutionary troops of the South of new Viet Nam.

One after another, from the cities to the rural areas, from the delta to the mountain regions, the elected *People's Committees* completely superseded the corrupt administrative machinery of mandarins and notables. In less than fifteen days, an entire new administrative machinery had been founded.

The prison doors were opened wide and political and common law prisoners were released by the revolutionary power; but traitors were severely punished. The head tax was abolished. The former fiscal regime was gradually modified. Land rents were reduced, and communal rice fields distributed more equitably. The French industrial enterprises, in the hands of the Japanese since March 9, 1945, passed into the control of the new power and were temporarily managed by the people or the Government. Democratic rights had been legally proclaimed and equality was to be practised regardless of nationality or sex. The republican regime with a new democratic character had been established.

With inconceivable strength, the whole Vietnamese people rose up and did their utmost to break the yoke imposed by the French and Japanese fascists, and resolutely went forward; side by side with the peoples of China and Indonesia, they marched in the vanguard of the Far-East peoples' liberation movement.

The resistance in Nam Bo

People's power had scarcely been founded in Viet Nam when the British forces and those of the Chinese Kuomintang, on the order of the Supreme Allied Command, landed in Indo-China to disarm the Japanese troops. The French colonialists in Indo-China had surrendered easily to the Japanese ; now relying on the British forces they prepared feverishly to recover their former position. And the most active of these French colonialists were precisely those fascists of the Petain-Decoux clique who were formerly the most zealous lackeys of the Japanese.

On September 23, armed and protected by the British forces, the French colonialists launched their attack and occupied Saigon. Our people replied by force of arms, and from that moment, our heroic resistance began. Since that time, our compatriots in South Viet Nam have endured hard trials, bearing almost all the weight of a revolutionary war which has enhanced the prestige of our people in the international arena, and set a good example to the smaller and weaker nations of the Far-East.

The Dong Nai * land, once drenched with the blood of the colonialist aggressors when they landed for the first time in our country, has today become a strong bulwark of the Fatherland. And continuing the tradition of heroes who, nearly one hundred years ago, sacrificed themselves to save the country, their descendants are today in the vanguard of the fight for the freedom and independence of our people.

---

* Dong Nai : name of a river in South Viet Nam. Dong Nai land Signifies Nam Bo (South Viet Nam).

Some essential remarks

Reviewing the history of the August Revolution, we can make some essential remarks.

First of all, the triumph of the August Revolution was due to the two following subjective and objective conditions :

Subjective condition : our people are united around the Viet Minh Front led by the Indochinese Communist Party. The proletarian class exercises this leadership without sharing it with any other class. It results from this that the revolutionary forces of our people are not scattered, that they have no rivalries or internal conflicts (except in some insignificant cases), and that at the decisive hour, they can be gathered together under the leadership of a single organisation to launch a direct and massive attack against the fortified enemy lines.

Objective condition : World War II created for the Vietnamese people an extremely favourable opportunity : the enemies of the Vietnamese Revolution, the Japanese and French fascists, had exhausted each other and grown weak. Moreover the Japanese were then defeated by the Soviet army ; that was enough for the Vietnamese people to fell them with a single blow and to seize power.

Yet, favourable though the objective conditions might have been, they could not have led to triumph without good subjective conditions. That is the truth.

Besides, the August Insurrection was a real revolution. The Vietnamese people, in bloody combat and with arms in their hands had to struggle against the Japanese fascists to regain their freedom and independence. Immediately after this, to defend these rights, they had to shed more blood. It is by the August Revolution that the dictatorial and fascist monarchical regimes have been overthrown and the democratic republican regime set up.

"History teaches us that a revolution has its particular features, the most important of which is the powerful uprising of masses who take their fate in their own hands and prepare the way to progress"

(Maurice Thorez — *A French policy*)

That is also an important characteristic of the August Revolution.[18]

---

[18] This chapter presents a generally accurate description of events. The Viet-Minh had fully understood the real importance of popular support, while the Japanese-supported imperial government and the Chinese-supported nationalists were helplessly bogged down in petty intrigues.

CHAPTER II

POLICY AND TACTICS OF THE VIETNAMESE COMMUNISTS IN THE AUGUST REVOLUTION[19]

More friends, less enemies

It is impossible to speak of the August Revolution without stressing the role of its leading core, the Viet Minh Front and the Indochinese Communist Party. The favourable opportunity was not enough to assure victory. A just policy and appropriate tactics were very much needed. Nor was the triumph of the general insurrection of August 19, 1945 due to mere chance.

From 1940, the Indochinese revolutionaries were facing two new facts : the world torn by war, the Indochinese people oppressed and exploited by the double yoke of the Japanese and French fascists. The national liberation policy advocated by the Viet Minh Front in the recent period was based on these two things.

The war threw into sharp relief the antagonism between the two belligerent camps. The double Japanese and French yoke united rich and poor, equally

---

[19] This chapter is a remarkably candid study of Communist tactics in riding the crest of a genuine "national liberation" movement.

hurt and humiliated, in the same hatred and the same struggle against the common enemy. At the same time, the conflicting interests of the Japanese and French who ruled Indo-China together, violently collided. One of the main tactics adopted by the Indochinese Communist Party and the Viet Minh Front in these recent years consisted in fully exploiting this situation.

That is why, in their foreign policy, the Indochinese Communist Party and the Viet Minh Front, realising that anti-fascist forces throughout the world were allies of the Vietnamese people, decided to side without reserve with the anti-fascist camp struggling for a just cause.

In its domestic policy, the Indochinese Communist Party organized the different strata of the people into the National Liberation Front : the Viet Minh Front. The programme of this Front assured the protection of human and civil rights and of property, the respect of private property, the liberty of conscience, as well as equality between nationalities and the sexes, with the aim of realising the unity of the whole people against the Japanese and French fascists. Facing the concrete conditions of the revolution in Indo-China, the Indo-chinese Communist Party, promoter and leader of the Viet Minh Front, left out of its programme the watch-word : Agrarian revolution, (deciding, for the present, not to confiscate land held by landlords), and this with a view to making a differentiation between types of landlords and winning a number of them over to the anti-imperialist cause, widening the National United Front to struggle for independence. This Front should comprise workers, peasants, petty-bourgeoisie of towns even national bourgeoisie, and include patriotic personalities belonging to the landlord class.

Besides this, the Indochinese Communist Party developed and consolidated in particular the peasants' and workers' organizations to give a solid base to the National United Front, and was determined to struggle against pro-French and pro-Japanese traitors.

On the one hand, the Party fully exploited the contradictions between the two enemies of our people — Japanese fascists and French colonialists in Indo-China — to give a vigorous impulse to the revolutionary movement, on the other hand, it tried every means to isolate the Japanese and French fascists.

When the fascists used repressive measures not only against Vietnamese revolutionaries but also against the progressive democratic French, the Party, in order to increase its own forces in the struggle against French and Japanese fascists, undertook to win over these French progressives to its cause, or at least to induce them to adopt a neutral attitude. When the French who had been overthrown by the Japanese, were no longer really dangerous enemies, the Party strove to unite its action with that of every French element ready to struggle against Japanese fascists.

In brief, the Party always saw clearly the principal and immediate enemy of the Revolution, doing its best to deprive the enemy of its supporters and to find new allies, never deviating from the aim of the National Liberation Revolution.

Flexibility of tactics

The Party had correctly foreseen that the Japanese and French would inevitably come into conflict, and had decided, should this happen, to change its tactics at once and immediately launch the general insurrection.

So, after the coup d'état of March 9, 1945, the Party launched a vast guerilla movement to seize local power and organized in the Highlands and Midlands of North Viet Nam model resistance bases against the Japanese. At the same time it changed its watchwords, forms of propaganda, organization and struggle so as to mobilize the masses more easily, and rapidly lead them towards the insurrection.

At that moment, the indispensable aim of propaganda consisted in unmasking the hypocrisy of the Japanese fascists and militarists and in destroying every illusion that it was expedient to use the Japanese and co-operate with them with a view to obtaining 'reforms' within the 'framework of legality' ... This only sowed confusion among the people toward the Japanese and their lackeys.

The propaganda used at that time took the ordinary form of speeches in factories, schools, markets, and public thoroughfares and the formation of shock teams by mobile groups who exhibited flags, banners and placards and distributed revolutionary documents.

A special propaganda form also used was the 'armed propaganda' with all its forms, including armed demonstrations and guerilla activities.

As for the agitation work, it took in hand the vital problem of the masses — to check famine — to lead the masses to seize Japanese rice stocks; according to the situation, these actions could be transformed into armed demonstrations.

The general form of struggle was the armed demonstration. Another special form used at this moment was the guerilla wherever the topography of the country was favourable, and yet another, the elimination of traitors in towns and country by *picked detachments*.

In organization, cleverness was used to transform the 'transitory organization' (temporary) into real organizations of the local people's power ; especially to develop the national salvation and self-defence groups (or guerilla troops) and organize the people's militia.

The general organizational forms were at that moment the association for national salvation, and especially the self-defence and combat groups.

The special forms were the *Viet Nam National Liberation Committee*, that is the provisional Government, *the People's Committee, and the Liberation Committees*. These Committees had at the same time an administrative, political and military character (that is a pre-governmental character), working in a determined period, simultaneously with the local administrative organisms founded by the Japanese and being transformed, after the general insurrection, into local official administrative organizations ; and lastly, the *National Insurrection Committee, the Action Committee* for each part of the country or each locality in the decisive hours, etc.

In brief, from March to August 1945, the tactics of the Party had the following characteristics :

First : to fully and at the correct time exploit the situation created by the Japanese coup d'état (March 9, 1945) in order immediately to lead the masses to new forms of struggle and organization of a higher degree ; to renounce the old methods, not to sit back facing the new situation, in other words, to know the importance of :

" *Putting in the forefront precisely those forms of struggle and organisation which are best suited to the conditions prevailing during the ebb or flow of the movement at a given moment, and which therefore can facilitate and ensure the bringing of the masses to the revolutionary positions, the bringing of the millions to the revolutionary front, and their disposition on the revolutionary front.*" (Stalin — *Principles of Leninism*).

In effect, after March 9, 1945, the forms of struggle such as armed propaganda, demonstrations followed by displays of force, sudden attacks against lonely posts and even the districts in the delta, suppression of the zealous agents of the Japanese fascists, organization of people's militia units even outside guerilla zones, etc. were so many bold blows showing the flexible character of the Party tactics. These tactics sowed confusion in the enemy ranks, developed the spirit of struggle for national salvation and the initiative of the masses, won over the waverers and quickly extended the movement for national salvation all over the country.

Second : in a given situation, to determine during the revolutionary work the fundamental task requiring immediate fulfilment in order to devote all forces to it and to accomplish it at any cost, because it is the best means to push the movement forward.

The insurrection of March 9, 1945 broke out when the famine was causing frightful ravages among the population. Hundreds of thousands of people starved beside granaries full of rice kept by the Japanese and French. At that moment a task of the greatest importance for the communist and Viet Minh cadres was to lead the armed masses to seize Japanese rice stores and French concessions full of stocks of agricultural produce. This had the result of inspiring organized and unorganized masses to take an active part in the movement against the Japanese, so that the more actively they struggled, the more they became conscious of their own strength and saw more clearly the real face of the enemy.

It was precisely thanks to these attacks on granaries and colonialist plantations that the national salvation movement could be developed intensely, the people rapidly armed, the self-defence brigades quickly founded where the movement had never been organized, and the Liberation Committees set up in numerous provinces. As Stalin said,

" The point here is to single out from all the problems confronting the Party that particular immediate problem, the answer to which constitutes the central point, and the solution of which will ensure the successful solution of the other immediate problems." (Stalin — *Principles of Leninism*).

Third : according to the situation, to use " transitory organization forms " such as *Revolutionary People's Committees, Revolutionary Workers' Committees, Local*

Liberation Committees, Viet Nam National Liberation Committee, progressively to gain on enemy power and paralyze its administrative machine. These organizations were very effective. They gave the people the occasion to realize universal suffrage and become acquainted with administrative affairs, led them to direct henceforth their own destiny, and break their chains themselves and ameliorate their living conditions by direct means, not paying attention to the power of the Japanese fascists and their lackeys. These " transitory organizations " mobilized the masses and encouraged them to participate in the revolutionary struggle ; they extended to the highest point the National United Front against the Japanese and created the bases for a new Viet Nam. In effect, after the August General Insurrection, these different Liberation Committees became real administrative organizations. To use People's Committees and Liberation Committees as springboards for the direct transition to the democratic republican regime, was an extremely interesting characteristic of the communist tactics in the pre-insurrectionary period.

The August Revolution won victories. Is that not due in great part to the intelligent and correct leadership of the Party ?

CHAPTER III

THE GOOD POINTS OF
THE AUGUST REVOLUTION

A careful preparation

The August Revolution victory was due in great part to the correct leadership of the Indochinese Communist Party, to its work of organization and preparation during the pre-insurrectionary period.

"In every revolution, victory does not come by itself, one must prepare it, win it." (Stalin). How did the Party prepare and win the victory of the August Revolution? It has exploited with cleverness favourable conditions created by the war to carry on fully the preparation of the insurrection. Here is this preparation plan in its main lines:

On the one hand, to unify the people's revolutionary forces, to mobilize manpower and wealth, to stimulate the ardent patriotism of the people, to adjust the different national salvation organizations, to lead the people in the struggle against white terror and for the defence of daily rights and interests.

On the other hand, to develop the para-military organizations such as the self-defence brigades, to

28

train military and political cadres, to procure arms, to organize the army, to establish the resistance zones, to carry out propaganda among the enemy soldiers, to train the people for destruction work and the tactics of scorched earth, etc., to launch guerilla warfare and seize power in different localities.

The documents of the Party and the Viet Minh Front such as *Preparations for the armed insurrection, Active preparations for the insurrection, Arms to expel the common enemy, Towards the general insurrection,* the pamphlets teaching *guerilla tactics,* etc . prove that, besides the psychological preparations we had to pay special attention to the material ones. The Party realized clearly that for the success of a revolution, the spirit of sacrifice is not enough, a meticulous military preparation is also needed : that is to say, the *founding of bases, the organizing of the regular army, the arming of the troops and the people.* As early as the end of 1941, the Party founded two bases, one at Bac Son — Dinh Ca (Lang Son - Thai Nguyen), and another at Cao Bang - Bac Can. *The Viet Nam Liberation Army* was founded during the struggle against the white terror in the Viet Bac (1941 - 1945); *the Viet Nam National Salvation Army,* still in an embryonic state at the time of the Bac Son insurrection (October 1940), developed through eight months of guerilla warfare waged at Dinh Ca and Trang Xa (August 1941 - April 1942), and in the second armed struggle at Dinh Ca (at the end of 1944)*. After the Japanese coup de force, the Ba To (Quang Ngai province) insurrection

---

* *In 1945, these two armies were unified and became "the Viet Nam Liberation Army".*[20]

[20] The Viet-Nam People's Army was officially created by Giap at Dinh Ca on December 22, 1944.

gave birth to another guerilla brigade. These forma-
tions played an extremely important role in the
*upsurge of the anti-Japanese fascist movement for national
salvation* and in *the August General Insurrection.*

A noticeable feature of the activity of the Party
in preparing for the armed insurrection is to have
made the masses conscious of the preparations for it
and led them to become active participants in it ;
simultaneously *to co-ordinate closely the military action
of guerilla brigades with the action of the masses, so that
the latter, while resisting the terror and struggling for the
defence of their rights and immediate interests, may feel
the necessity of taking up arms to win national independence.* The struggles against the concentration of villages, arrests, requisitions of paddy, forced enlistments
and conscription of labourers, crop destructions for
the cultivation of jute, the pillage of markets, etc.
had hastened the arming and training of the masses
for a bold march towards the insurrection.

The preparation, meticulous and in conformity
with principle, was one of the good points of the
August Revolution.

Promptness and timeliness

The victory of an insurrection depends not only
on careful preparation, but also on its timely launching.

As we have seen, the August Revolution took
place at a very good time.

If on March 9, 1945, the general insurrection had
broken out immediately after the Japanese coup de

force, the Revolution could have lost much and power could not have been established all over the country, because where the revolutionary forces were weak, the Japanese forces, still strong at that moment, would have been able to destroy them. That is why the insurrection was launched only in small areas to conquer local power. However, if after the Japanese surrender, our people had passively waited for the coming of the Allied forces to " liberate " them without rising immediately to conquer power all over the country, what would have happened then ? Two possibilities could have occurred : either the Japanese lackeys would have come on to the stage to solemnly boast of " having no more links with the Japanese " and to parade themselves as the " defenders of independence and democracy ", not for liberating the people, but for surrendering to the Anglo-Americans. Or the French would have tried to raise their heads again, gather the remnants of their forces in Indo-China, call back the debris of the troops who had fled to China after the blow of March 9, which would have allowed them to found, with the participation of the pro - French traitors, a puppet government over the whole country, and to declare that they had implemented the Proclamation of March 24, 1945, and given autonomy to Indo-China *.

Both these eventualities would have created the same fatal consequences for our country.

---

* It was only after the French surrender in Indo-China that the de Gaulle Government agreed to issue the Proclamation recognizing the autonomy of Indo-China. This hypocritical proclamation was, for the Indochinese peoples, as stupid as it was ridiculous because it was published just at the time when the French had no more authority in Indo-China.

But fortunately the Party had led the people's struggle for national salvation and effectively created favourable conditions for the victory of the August Revolution. And just before the Japanese defeat (August 13, 1945), it immediately issued the general insurrection order to conquer power from the Japanese without the least hesitation or weakness, to organise people's power, and thanks to the revolutionary forces of the masses to bundle out the so-called " autonomy " proposed by the French!

The leaders of the August Revolution had " *Well chosen the moment for the decisive blow, the moment for starting the insurrection, so timed as to coincide with the moment when the crisis has reached its climax, when it is fully apparent that the vanguard is pre-pared to fight to the end, the reserves are prepared to support the vanguard, and maximum consternation reigns in the ranks of the enemy.* " (Stalin — *Principles of Leninism*).

Promptitude and timeliness, that is another good point of the August Revolution.

The whole people rose up

The victory of the August Revolution was also due to the unity of the whole people and the rising up of the masses.

Truly, the August Revolution induced the great majority of the people to rise up and paralyze entirely the reactionary elements. This is a fact of great import-ance. If the general insurrection had not won the whole people:

First, the French colonialists could have found a way out ; they would have won and exploited the elements unfavourable to the Revolution, and basing themselves on the latter's attitude, would have been able to declare before the U.N.O. and the world that the Vietnamese people welcomed the restoration of their power ; at the same time they would have accused the forces of insurrection, as being " rebellious elements ", preventing them from disarming the Japanese troops and restoring order and peace in Indo-China, etc.

Second : the international reactionary elements in general, could have exploited our lack of unity to dig still deeper the ditch between the various strata of our people. Worse still, they could have provoked a civil war, plunged the country into division and anarchy and worn out our forces so as to dominate us easily.

But fortunately, our people, wretched under the double yoke of oppression and exploitation of the Japanese and French fascists, closed their ranks under the gold starred red flag and, relying on their own forces, rose up to win back their liberty.

In August 1945, the *Dai Viet* * clique allied to the reactionary elements of the Viet Nam Quoc Dan Dang Party ** and the Phuc Quoc * clique asked the Japanese to give them the administrative power in some places (such as Vinh Yen, Mong Cai etc.), to stand up against the *Republican Government*. But their shabby behaviour as lackeys of a foreign country was

---

* *Dai Viet : Great Viet Nam.*

Phuc Quoc : National Restoration ; two pro-Japanese traitorous organizations,

** *Viet Nam Quoc Dan Dang : Viet Nam Nationalist Party, (a Party which was against the Viet Minh).*

so obvious that the whole people had the most profound contempt for them, and their influence, far from extending, withered away.

An overall rising by the entire people, such is the third good point of the August Revolution.

These three good points were entirely due to the powerful organized forces and the correct political line of the *Indochinese Communist Party* and of *the Viet Minh Front.*

We can say that without the Indochinese Communist Party and the Viet Minh Front, the Revolution would have taken another road. If the Viet Minh could not have unified all social classes, had not had prestige among the masses and had not led the insurrection for the conquest of power, the Revolution could have failed.

The former liberation movements of our predecessors against the French failed. One of the main causes of this defeat was the lack of an anti-colonialist united national front. Those former insurrections were crushed, principally because they were the rising of only a sect, a group of militants, or a little vanguard detachment and not " a far-reaching and deep-rooted revolution of the people " (Stalin). To triumph, a revolution worthy of new times must be a real revolution of the broad masses, prepared and led by one or several revolutionary organizations. The August Revolution conquered power, the direct aim of every revolution, because it was the work of a whole people united in the struggle under the leadership of the Indochinese Communist Party.

CHAPTER IV

THE WEAKNESSES
OF THE AUGUST REVOLUTION

Unequal degree of determination
throughout the country

Besides these good points, has the August Revolution any weak ones ? Yes, it has.

First, the general insurrection was not launched with the same resolution throughout the three " Kys " *, this does not mean that the uprisings should have been carried out in one sweep throughout the whole country. Such an event would present many difficulties because in an agricultural country like Viet Nam, the degree of political consciousness and organizational spirit of the people are at different levels in different places and means of communication are still backward. But in the conditions prevailing in our country in August last year, it would have been better to launch the uprisings simultaneously in the main towns, which would allow a more decisive and better managed seizing of power and would end by robbing the French

---

* *Viet Nam was divided by the French into three parts, the three " Kys "* [21]

[21] It was not the French-administered but the pre-French independent Viet-Nam that was divided into three *ky* (parts). The D.R.V.N. uses the expression *bo* (sections) to designate those same three areas.

colonialists of all hope. Now, whereas the insurrection was launched simultaneously in many places in the first week following the Japanese surrender, Saigon waited until the 23rd to rise up. Nam Bo was a little late because among the ranks of the army of insurrection in the South, there were many elements who did not believe in the strength of the masses and would rather have used plain diplomacy to persuade the Japanese to give us power than struggle by their own forces to wrest it back or support the diplomatic work with action by the armed masses. Furthermore, they feared the crushing of such an uprising by the Japanese forces, forgetting that the latter were already almost paralysed at that moment and would be even more paralysed before the strong, broad masses of the whole nation.

This weakness is due to the unequal development of the Vietnamese Revolution as well as to the relative weakness of the Viet Minh organization in Nam Bo before the zero hour of the insurrection and to the lack of homogeneity in the ranks of the United National Front in the South. Another reason is that Nam Bo is situated far from the national leading organism *, a fact that proved detrimental to the judiciousness of the instructions given by the Viet Minh in the South, preventing them from entirely keeping pace with the general line of the Party. In the South, the slowness in starting the insurrection,

---

* At that time, the Central Committee of the Indochinese Communist Party and the Central Bureau of the Viet Minh had their headquarters in Bac Bo (Northern part of Viet Nam).

the lack of resolution in the seizing of power, encouraged the reactionaries, especially the French colonialists and pro-French Vietnamese traitors.

Lack of full disarmament of the Japanese troops

The second weakness in the August Revolution was the failure to fully disarm the Japanese troops at the hour of the insurrection before the entry of the Allies into the country.[22]

This task *was carried out* to a certain extent. But even in many places where our forces prevailed over those of the enemy, we did not use violence to disarm the Japanese; moreover, we did not even cause them any trouble when they remained neutral and let us organize the people's power. Generally speaking, under the circumstances of August last year, that policy was correct, because the revolutionaries have no right to waste the masses' blood and throw themselves into hazardous undertakings, out of mere conceit. Our weakness did not consist in negotiating with the Japanese, but in failing to make the fullest use of the armed masses to support the diplomatic action and force the Japanese to surrender more weapons; furthermore, we did not act in time to prevent them from destroying a great many up-to-date armaments.

Now, each time we consider the lack of modern arms, we cannot in retrospect help regretting that in many places, the insurrection troops missed a very rare opportunity to secure the necessary weapons.

[22] Although the Viet-Minh did not seize all Japanese equipment in Viet-Nam, it nevertheless succeeded in obtaining 35,000 rifles, 1,350 automatic weapons, 200 mortars, 54 cannon, and even 18 tanks from Japanese sources, French booty stocks, and American airdrops. This should dispose of the myth that the Viet-Minh began the war against the French almost barehanded.

The pro-Japanese puppets have repeatedly upbraided the Viet Minh for behaving too harshly towards the Japanese and killing many of them in various places, thus provoking them to destroy many good quality weapons. These "good" people asserted that, in the conditions prevailing last August, if the Viet Minh had not intervened, they would have been able to "negotiate" with the Japanese and get many arms from them within a few days. We regret having to put it to these gentlemen: if the Viet Minh had not led the whole people in the general insurrection, permitting them quickly to seize a portion of the Japanese arms held by the "Bao An" units and Japanese troops, when these "gentlemen" expected to be given these "begged-for" arms by the Japanese; and if they had succeeded in getting them, we can be sure they would have used them with an object other than establishing and consolidating the democratic republican system and the people's power, or expelling the foreign aggression and checking the counter-revolution!

This failure to completely disarm the Japanese troops was due to the subjective conditions of the August Revolution. In plain words, when you have only a small capital, you cannot expect to make big profits: and without tanks and heavy guns, we could not take possession of the Japanese tanks and heavy guns. What happened was that in many regions, immediately after the insurrectional forces had occupied a town, either by a sudden attack from outside or by an inner uprising, the Japanese entrenched themselves in their blockhouses and made ready to defend themselves; and while they had enough supplies and munitions to hold out for a long time, our troops merely encircled them and, for want of good tactics, failed to destroy their fortifications (as for example, the seizure of Thai Nguyen); whatever the case, it must be admitted that with more promptitude and boldness, we should have been able to disarm the Japanese troops from the very beginning of the insurrection, Were not the insurrection troops successful in many places without any bloodshed or hard fighting? It seemed that the forces of insurrection were breaking a butterfly on the wheel : faced with an exhausted and already defeated enemy, they failed to avail themselves of the situation and, by taking a further step, should have been able to snatch the weapons from the hands of the Japanese. For in fact, our military task in that period consisted more in disarming the enemy than in casting him down.

That shortcoming is one of the reasons why the August Revolution did not take on as heroic a character as that of the great revolutions in other countries.

Lack of firmness in the repression of counter-revolutionary elements

Here is the third weakness of the August Revolution. Immediately after the establishment of revolutionary power, we did not firmly eliminate the various categories of traitors and failed to take sufficiently energetic measures against the French colonialists and their agents. Only in some regions such as in Quang Ngai did the forces of insurrection carry out the policy of " Sweeping away all reactionaries ", but they did it in an extremist way ; almost everywhere else we were conciliatory to the point of weakness, forgetting that " a victorious power must be a dictatorial one. " (Lenin)

The more democratic the power, the more dictatorial it must be — that is, it must exercise the democratic dictatorship of the whole people against the very small reactionary minority ready to grab back their age-old domination and hinder the march of the revolution. Not being firmly repressed, the reactionaries at home have been used by the French and international reactionaries to create difficulties for the revolutionary power and to divide our people. One wonders why the Administrative Committee of Nam Bo immediately after its foundation, did not order the immediate arrest of the pro-French Nguyen Van Thinh traitors, some of the most dangerous and mischievous elements among the pro-Japanese, and the most confirmed trotskyite, sabotage experts, which fact allowed these people to prepare the return of the French by creating provocations before and on Independence Day (Sept. 2, 1945)? One wonders why in Bac Bo, after the foundation of the people's power in the capital, many pro-Japanese traitors and other Machiavellian agents from abroad were not arrested ?

We admit that, because of the extremely intricate situation of our country and the relatively limited strength of the Vietnamese Revolution, it was not possible to carry out a systematic elimination of the counter-revolutionary elements on Jacobean or Bolshevik lines. The Vietnamese Revolution was not opposing only the counter-revolutionary forces at home; other forces were intervening from abroad in favour of the French reactionaries and other traitors. It was due to this that the latter were able, in certain places, and at certain moments, to equal, and even to overpower the revolutionary forces (in Saigon, for example).

However, it is to be regretted that energetic, timely and necessary measures to counteract all possible dangers in the future were not taken immediately upon the seizing of power and before any foreign intervention, at a time when the reactionaries in the country were still at a loss and had no time to reorganize themselves. This does not mean that after the general insurrection, we should have imprisoned all the French, or put to death all elements who had collaborated in any way with the French or the Japanese. No! We regret only that the repression of the reactionaries during the August Revolution was not carried out fully within the framework of its possibilities.

Revolutionary power should willingly pardon the guilty who repent but it must be firm with all traitors.

For a new-born revolutionary power to be lenient with counter-revolutionaries is tantamount to committing suicide. Did not the Paris Commune commit a grave error in failing to pursue and eliminate the " Versaillais " ?

Failure to seize the Bank of Indo-China

The fourth shortcoming of the August Revolution : the forces of insurrection failed to seize the Bank of Indo-China and suppress the privileges of the magnates of the money-market in Indo-China ; moreover, they failed even to gain control of the Bank. The colonialists availed themselves of this opportunity to attack us later on in the financial·field : as for example by the rejection of 500-piastre notes, thus placing more difficulties in our path. In the same way, the Paris Commune met with so many obstacles precisely because it failed to seize hold of the Bank of France.

The Japanese and the French bequeathed to our people's power an almost hopeless economic and financial heritage. But we were able to hold our own because of the sacrifices made by our workers, public servants and soldiers, and because of the industrious and devoted efforts of the government and the whole people.

This fourth shortcoming was not due to any underestimation by the leaders of the August Revolution of the financial question, but due rather to the fact that the Bank of Indo-China is a financial institution acting not only on behalf of the French and the Japanese but also of other countries.

If we were not able to sweep away all the French imperialists in one blow, how could we hold out firmly against several other imperialists as well ?

The four above-mentioned shortcomings of the August Revolution had their reasons. But, in an objective criticism, we cannot fail to point them out frankly.

We admit that, for one reason or the other and taking into account the conditions of the August Revolution, it was difficult to avoid them. But the error [23] of our revolutionaries consisted in failing to avail themselves of the high tide of the revolutionary movement and of the people's spirit of sacrifice in the decisive hours so as to reduce to a minimum the extent of these shortcomings.

[23] This is an open criticism of Ho Chi Minh's policy of attempting to negotiate a settlement with France precisely when this article came out in the Hanoi newspaper *Su-That*.

CHAPTER V

CHARACTER AND SIGNIFICANCE OF THE AUGUST REVOLUTION

Character of the August Revolution

The August Revolution was a revolution for national liberation. It aimed at liberating the Vietnamese people from the colonial yoke and making Viet Nam an independent nation.

However, because it struggled against the Japanese and French fascists as well as their lackeys, the feudal reactionaries, and because it contributed a part, though small, in the great world anti-fascist struggle, it had the character of a democratic revolution, though it has not abolished all the vestiges of feudalism in Viet Nam, nor realised agrarian reform so as to distribute the land held by the landlords to the peasants.

In the present historic conditions, a colonial revolution must have the following double character: first, it must be an *anti-imperialist revolution* aimed at overthrowing the imperialist domination, and second, it must be an *agrarian revolution* so as to confiscate the lands of the feudal landlords and distribute them to the peasants. The August Revolution

44

has only aimed at overthrowing the imperialist rule and that of the feudal puppets, and setting up the democratic republican regime ; but it has not abolished land ownership by the feudal landlord class and all other vestiges of feudalism to create conditions for industrial and commercial development. Thanks to the August Revolution, a portion of the imperialists' and traitors' lands have been confiscated, land rents have been reduced by 25 per cent and some of the old compound-interested debts have been cancelled. However, in the agrarian field, generally speaking, the relations between landlords and peasants have not changed. Therefore we can say that, though the August Revolution has a democratic character, this character is not strongly marked enough.

Some people have said that, because the August Revolution has abolished the Imperial Government with its machinery composed of mandarins and notables, it has a distinctly anti-feudal character. But by abolishing the Imperial Government, we have abolished only one aspect of the feudal regime ; because its basis, which is rooted now in the relations between landlords and peasants in the agrarian field, is still alive, the feudal regime is still in existence. We must see to it that we advance the anti-feudal struggle, and not be complacent about the achievements of the August Revolution.

It is clear that the August Revolution has established in Viet Nam a democratic republican having the character of a new democracy. Popular representation has been widely established at all levels by universal suffrage ; complete equality between the

sexes, wide democratic freedoms, as well as personal
liberty and equality b tween all nationalities big and
small, have been promulgated ; the regime of popular
assembly, ensuring the legislative and executive powers
of the people, has been established and there exists a
democratic regime completely different from bourgeois
parliamentary democracy, which grants the people
only limited rights in making proposals and in criti-
cizing the government ; the State economic sector is
taking shape ; the people's conditions of life are improved ; attention is paid to the life of the worker
and peasant masses ; the 8-hour working day is officially recognized ; the proletarian class now actually
holds power, etc. All these facts make it amply clear
that the Vietnamese regime is that of a democratic
republic of a new style quite different from the old-
style bourgeois democratic regime (for example the
French bourgeois parliamentary regime). However, the
democratic regime in Viet Nam is different from the
present Soviet democratic regime. Indeed, the democratic regime in Viet Nam guarantees the interests of
all social strata, while the parliamentary republican
regime in France is a disguised dictatorship of the
bourgeoisie : under the cloak of democracy the bourgeois class exerts a dictatorial power which defends
only the interests of a minority of exploiters, the
capitalists. As for the Soviet democratic republican
regime, it is a regime, in which the proletarian class
officially exercises the dictatorship, suppresses all vestiges of the exploiting class (landlords, bourgeois and
kulaks) and guarantees the widest interests of all
labouring people (workers, peasants, intellectuals) who

liberated themselves and are co-operating to build a new life under the leadership of the proletarian class.

The republican democratic regime in Viet Nam is in keeping with the stage of development of our country and with the present world democratic movement. Though it has been established in a backward agricultural country, it carries a new and progressive character, because it was born of the hard and fierce struggle against the French and Japanese fascists, out of the struggle for national liberation led by the proletarian class. A struggle led by the most revolutionary class against the most reactionary enemy must be crowned with the installation of a non-conservative regime, quite the reverse of the retrograde regime of the enemy. Moreover, if our regime has the character of a new democracy, that is because it was born at a time when the vanguard democratic regime of the Soviet Union has fully triumphed over its enemies, and is being consolidated after surviving the terrible test of war, after the collapse of the world system of fascism, and while the great movement of progressive democracy is spreading throughout the world. Born in the new times, the democratic republican regime in Viet Nam inevitably bears the mark of the new times. The August Revolution is a revolution of national liberation in its form and one of new democracy in its content. In other words, the August Revolution is a revolution of national liberation with a new democratic character. It constitutes a step in the national democratic revolution of Viet Nam.

The historic significance of the August Revolution

The August Revolution has highlighted the indomitable spirit of the Vietnamese people, a people who are struggling untiringly to shake off the foreign yoke. It is the completion of 80 years of uninterrupted struggle of the Vietnamese people against the French colonialists. It also constitutes the greatest historic event in our country since the victory gained by Quang Trung who drove the Manchu troops out of Viet Nam in 1789. In fact, since then there has been no national movement which has, as fully as the August Revolution, given evidence of the indomitable heroism and of the strong unity of the Vietnamese people. It has not merely broken the double yoke imposed by the Japanese and the French, but it has also overthrown the monarchic regime established for thousands of years in Viet Nam, changed the country into a new democratic republic, promoting the Vietnamese people to the rank of a vanguard people. Therein lies the great significance of the August Revolution ; and President Ho Chi Minh, the first President of the Democratic Republic of Viet Nam, the leader of the August Revolution, thoroughly deserves the title of national hero.

Through the August Revolution, the Vietnamese people have clearly shown their anti-fascist spirit and their attachment to democracy and peace. The revolution constitutes the splendid completion of the great movement against the French and Japanese fascists in Viet Nam during World War II, especially from March last year. Before the August Revolution, the Vietnamese people struggled in very hard conditions to harass and exhaust the rear lines of the Japanese forces. From the end of 1944, the Japanese sea-lines were attacked by the Allied forces; Indo-China had become a "bridge" over the Japanese "Great Oriental Asia Road", a bridge extremely important for the movement and supply of Japanese troops from the Northern position to Indonesia. The blocking of this bridge to the Japanese forces was the task assumed by the Vietnamese people. Therefore, in March 1945, the Indochinese Communist Party launched the great movement of struggle against the Japanese for national salvation, by organizing and actively leading the Vietnamese people to the attack on important Japanese strategic positions, thus causing a block in the traffic of the Japanese over the "Great Oriental Asia" road.

From March to August last year, Japanese territory suffered more and more violent bombing raids. In Indo-China, the Vietnamese guerillas were fighting the Japanese with increased strength. A free zone was established in the Highlands and Midlands of North Viet Nam and constituted a permanent obstacle on the path of the Japanese from Southern China to Indo-China. In this zone, the guerillas exhausted the Japanese forces, not allowing them a moment's respite. In this way the Vietnamese people had effectively contributed their part, beside the Allies, to speed the overthrow of the Japanese and indirectly, to hasten the Soviet army's victory. It is an indubitable fact that the Vietnamese people have made their share of sacrifices in the struggle against the fascist aggressors during the recent years.

The French reactionary colonialists purposely call
the August Revolution "pro-Japanese", "Japanese-
led" to belittle its significance. But there is plenty
of evidence to smash their treacherous slanders. Today
everybody has to admit that the reactionary attitude
of the French colonialists with regard to the August
Revolution is that of the robber who loots and at the
same time cries "Stop thief". In point of fact, did not
the French colonialists, assisted by the British imperialists, make use of the Japanese troops to counter-
attack the Vietnamese Revolution ?

Among the peoples oppressed by the Japanese,
the Indonesian, Chinese and Vietnamese peoples have
been the most successful in availing themselves of the
Japanese capitulation last August to rise up and win
democracy and freedom *.

By the fact of the August Revolution, the Vietnamese people have lodged this general claim to the
U.N.O. : *the Great Powers must recognize the right to self-
determination of the Vietnamese people, in accordance
with the Atlantic and San Francisco Charters.* As a
natural consequence of the Japanese collapse, all
peoples under the Japanese yoke must be liberated,
and nobody must be allowed to replace the Japanese
in oppressing and exploiting them. The Vietnamese

---

* *The peoples of Burma, Malaya and the Philippines also organized guerilla forces to resist the Japanese invaders but when the Japanese
surrendered, their forces were still insufficient to cope with the invasion
of the U.S. and British imperialists, who were more powerful than their
congeners, the French and the Dutch. Therefore, in spite of their relatively
big efforts and sacrifices, their struggles have not brought as important
results as those obtained by the peoples of Indonesia, China and Viet Nam.*

people have suffered from Japanese domination since 1940 and they have worthily played their part side by side with the Allies in the struggle against the Japanese, thus they fully deserve their independence. The Vietnamese people will resolutely oppose the return of the French oppressors as well as the regime of a "mandated country", because they have already attained their majority.

The August Revolution and the war of self-defence waged for almost a year by the Vietnamese people against the French reactionaries have proclaimed these eager aspirations to the world. They show clearly that the colonial imperialist system is disintegrating and that the hour of liberation has struck for the oppressed peoples. The Vietnamese Revolution, like the Chinese and Indonesian Revolutions, strongly promotes the liberation movements of the Laotian and Cambodian peoples and other colonial countries in South-East Asia : this fact explains clearly why the British imperialists have done their best to help the French colonialists to repress the Vietnamese Revolution in South Viet Nam and why the international reactionaries have made concessions to one another to allow the French to relieve the troops of Chiang Kai-shek in North Viet Nam.[24]

In fact, from September 23 last year and all through our struggle waged against the French, our forces have met the British, Indian, French and Japanese troops in many a battle. Our struggle of self-defence has unveiled the perfidious schemes of the international reactionaries. It has exposed before world opinion that from the start of their landing in Indo-China, the

[24] The French had begun negotiations with Chungking late in 1945 in order to obtain the withdrawal of Chinese Nationalist forces from Indochina north of the 16th parallel. The Chinese finally agreed in February, 1946, after the French surrendered all their special rights and privileges in China. Prior to their departure, the Chinese sold Ho many of the brand-new American weapons and other equipment they had received in 1943–45.

British troops, only commissioned by the Allies to disarm and repatriate the Japanese soldiers, instead of setting to this task of repatriation, used these soldiers to help the French colonialists to counter-attack the Vietnamese Revolution and repress the Vietnamese people's struggle of self-defence ; thus, we can say that *the Vietnamese people are not fighting for themselves only, but also to a certain degree, for the defence of world peace.*

At the end of the anti-fascist war, the task of all progressive world forces is to develop democracy and build peace. With the August Revolution and the present Resistance War, the Vietnamese people have shouldered a part of the responsibility to fulfil this mission side by side with the progressive and democratic forces struggling for a better world. Whether one likes it or not, the August Revolution is part of the great movement of mankind for the building of peace and democracy. The Vietnamese people fully understand their international role in this post-war period. They are determined to fulfil this task, whatever the obstacles may be !

This is precisely the reason why the August Revolution is warmly acclaimed by progressive opinion and why the Vietnamese people now enjoy tokens of solidarity and sympathy from all democratic countries throughout the world, especially from the oppressed peoples.

CHAPTER VI

PROSPECTS OF
THE VIETNAMESE REVOLUTION

Favourable conditions
of the Vietnamese Revolution

What conditions will advance the Vietnamese Revolution and ensure its final victory?

Here are two important conditions:

First, subjectively speaking, the Vietnamese people, weighted for a long time under the French yoke and recently by the double oppression and exploitation of the French and Japanese fascists, have realized that only Revolution can liberate them. Closely united under the national banner they are determined to support the Republican Government in national liberation and national reform. The National United Front, under the remarkable leadership of President Ho Chi Minh and with the bloc of national salvation and democracy — the Viet Minh — as its base, will certainly achieve its duty of mobilizing the whole people to counter all reactionary forces, overcome all difficulties and obstacles and march forward.

Secondly, from the objective point of view, since World War II the international situation has brought new prospects to the Vietnamese Revolution: the Soviet Union, completely victorious, has become an invincible force. In several countries, the Communist Party has organized power or taken part in it, new democratic movements are developing in many countries, especially in those just liberated from the fascist yoke; the movement for national liberation is boiling up in colonial and semi-colonial countries. After the collapse of fascism, the imperialist system has grown weak. The movement for the consolidation of peace against international reaction has attracted the majority of mankind. The Vietnamese Revolution, as part of the world movement of peace and democracy, is inevitably deeply influenced by the international progressive movement.

The Vietnamese Revolution also stands between the revolutionary streams of China, Indonesia and India, from which it receives a good influence and with which it is in tune; at the same time the Vietnamese revolution exerts a considerable influence upon those movements.

In short, the Vietnamese Revolution has sufficient conditions to march forward strongly to final victory.

Objectives to be achieved

Nevertheless, no matter how important the achievements of the August Revolution are at present, we must recognize this objective truth: the national liberation of Viet Nam has not yet completely succeeded.

The August Revolution seized power for the people, but from September 23, 1945, the French colonialists attacked us and partly wrested it back. In the South of Viet Nam, they set up the puppet government under Nguyen Van Thinh and re-established their domination in some towns. According to the Preliminary Agreement of March 6, 1946, Viet Nam and France came to a compromise : France agreed to recognize Viet Nam as a free State having its own Government, its Parliament, its army and its own system of finance ; Viet Nam agreed to remain part of the French Union ; French troops were given the right to be stationed on the territory of Viet Nam for a fixed period, and generally speaking, French economic and cultural interests in Viet Nam are to be ensured. So, our country is only a free State, but not yet a completely independent one.

What is complete independence ? The whole of Viet Nam from Muc Nam Quan to Ca Mau must be placed under the people's power organized by the people ; there should be no foreign troops on the territory of Viet Nam ; Vietnamese economy must be independent, not tied to French economy or to that of any country ; Viet Nam must develop its national culture. In a word, the Vietnamese people must be the masters of their country in every respect and the Revolution for national liberation must complete its task of shattering all imperialist bonds.

The Franco-Vietnamese Preliminary Agreement as well as the Franco-Vietnamese treaty which may be signed soon are not ultimate aims but only temporary measures in order to give our people a moment's breathing space in which to consolidate the position of the democratic republican regime brought into being by the August Revolution, to strengthen our real forces to march towards a new stage.[25]

The Vietnamese Revolution must unceasingly progress, sometimes quickly, sometimes slowly, sometimes by leaps and bounds, sometimes stopping for a time to regain breath, or move a step backwards to jump across a deep ditch, sometimes dodging to avoid an obstacle so as to reach rapidly its goal.

During the course of its development, the Vietnamese Revolution must not only fulfil its anti-imperialist task but also complete its anti-feudal task which is land reform. Because so long as these tasks are not realized, Viet Nam will not get rid of its backwardness and become really strong and prosperous; so long as these tasks are not realized, people's happiness cannot be guaranteed.

Indeed, to become prosperous and happy, Viet Nam, now an agricultural country, must change into an industrial one (because only with a developed industry can a country produce sufficient arms for its national defence and sufficient goods for the people's well-being). But the long imperialist domination has always kept Viet Nam in a backward agricultural State. The French imperialists monopolized heavy industry for French capitalists in France and established only light industry in Indo-China. In the development of small industry, the capitalists of our country suffered from imperialist competition, while under the French and Japanese domination, the question of installing heavy industry was far beyond their reach. Thus, the French imperialists monopolized heavy industry with

---

[25] This is the gist of the "Brest-Litovsk Doctrine" that Truong Chinh and Giap were then expounding: Sign anything in order to stall for time.

the aim of compelling Viet Nam to consume their goods and preventing all competition with them. How can an essentially agricultural country compete with a country which has a developed heavy industry ? It cannot. That is why, to become a prosperous country, Viet Nam must get free of all imperialist links and develop its heavy industry, so as to be completely liberated from foreign economic subordination. This means that it must be independent in the economic field as well as in political and cultural fields. The Vietnamese Revolution has not yet thoroughly abolished all imperialist privileges from our country, but has only restricted them. It must progress further to fulfil its anti-imperialist task.

In the other field, the French imperialists continued to maintain all forms of feudal exploitation to make use of them in order to exploit our people more and more. In the mountainous regions, even today, they continue to carry out serfdom and forced labour. In the delta, the tenancy regime with high land rents is still maintained. Moreover there are still heavy taxes and requisitioning, side by side with many privileges for a few. Most of the people are peasants and they are cruelly exploited, and as a result, many of them have become impoverished ; they cannot continue to live in the countryside and have to go to the towns hoping to find jobs in factories ; but as industry in our country cannot develop, the few enterprises which exist (factories, mines, plantations, etc.) can only employ a small number of these people while the remainder go to increase the ranks of the " Reserve army for industry ", in other words, the army of unemployed or vagrants. The greater the number of unemployed, the lower the wages. The very low wages have a considerable influence on technical improvement in agriculture and industry. As the exploitation of cheap labour was sufficient for their own interests, the colonialists did not bother to improve production techniques, and as a result, the economy of Viet Nam under the imperalist yoke was unable to escape from a vicious backward circle. The Vietnamese peasants are still short of land to till and the workers heavily exploited. In an agricultural country like ours, in speaking of the people's happiness, we must speak of the improvement of the peasants' and workers' life, particularly when nearly 90 per cent of the people are peasants. But how can the peasants' living conditions be effectively improved if they have not enough land to till? Therefore, the question of the people's happiness is basically one of giving land to the peasants.

Finally, for this reason, the regime of feudal and semi-feudal exploitation must be abolished, and " land to the tillers " must be realized. So far, the Vietnamese Revolution has only restricted that feudal and semi-feudal exploitation. It must progress further to realise land reform and wipe out all vestiges of feudalism. In brief, the Vietnamese Revolution must fulfil both the anti-imperialist and anti-feudal tasks to realize independence, freedom and happiness for the people. In other words, it must complete the task of democratization to pave the way to the socialist revolution in the future : to socialize all means of production, abolish from Viet Nam the regime of exploitation of man by man.

Process of development of the Vietnamese
Revolution

The wrong conception of the progress of the Vietnamese Revolution must be wiped out now. People think that the Vietnamese Revolution must progress step by step: that after the revolution of national liberation (anti-imperialist) comes the agrarian revolution (anti-feudal), then the socialist revolution.

This theory of "successive progression" according to a fixed plan, cutting the Vietnamese Revolution into three stages, is not right. Abroad, the Soviet Union, the socialist State, has triumphed and the new democratic movement is in full development. At home, the leadership of the Vietnamese Revolution grows stronger and stronger in *the hands of the proletarian class in power;* the progressive democratic forces form an unshakable bloc. In such historic conditions, the Revolution for the national liberation of Viet Nam can fulfil its anti-imperialist task and at the same time *realize a part* of the agrarian task. The Vietnamese democratic revolution does not have to wait for a determined date before it breaks out, but can be realized in the course itself of the development of new democracy in Viet Nam, a development which may be rapid thanks to the support of the new democratic movement throughout the world (particularly in China and in France); and because the movement for the socialist revolution is growing steadily all over the world, the Vietnamese socialist Revolution may also be achieved even if it has not all the necessary social conditions (for instance : heavy industry is not yet developed, all forms of small capitalist exploitation are not yet abolished etc.) As is stated in the Communist International Programme:

"...Although the social relations of every colony and semi-colony have not yet ripened, all movements for national liberation in these countries can also develop into socialism, if these movements enjoy, in particular, the help and support of proletarian dictatorship and in general, that of the international proletarian movement."

CHAPTER VII

THE URGENT TASKS OF THE VIETNAMESE PEOPLE

Four chief points, four slogans

After the second world war, the Vietnamese Revolution, developing in the new conditions prevailing in the world, has several allies and enjoys much support. But no matter how favourable conditions are, the Revolution might fail if our people, and especially our revolutionary fighters, were to go the wrong way.

Moreover, the French reactionaries, collaborating with the international reactionaries, are carrying out a perfidious policy designed to rob us of our power... Officially, they recognize our country as a free State, but in actual fact, they want to make of our country an autonomous one.

Under the cover of " New France ", they have signed an agreement with us, but at the same time they use fascist methods which run counter to the French people's will : indulging in acts of provocation, acts of " faits accomplis ", and gradual encroachment, so that finally the " Agreement " becomes a worthless scrap of paper.

Cunningly and according to a systematic plan, they apply the traditional imperialist policy, of " divide and rule ": territorial parcelling, division between different nationalities, religions, political parties, etc. aimed at rendering us powerless to fight against them. They savagely terrorize people in the occupied zones or in the zones where their strength is greater than ours, hoping to annihilate our cadres and to intimidate and demoralize our compatriots.

We are faced with a Machiavellian and experienced enemy. New difficulties await us. All our compatriots must remain most vigilant and thoroughly understand their urgent task.

What is the aim of our people in the present stage? In our opinion, our people's task can be summed up in these four chief points :

INDEPENDENCE, UNIFICATION, DEMOCRACY, RENAISSANCE

a) *INDEPENDENCE :* Our country is not yet completely independent. The foreign army is still on our territory. We must struggle to force them to withdraw from our country in the near future. We must struggle for our national sovereignty, so that in addition to our own government, army, finances, and Parliament, we also have our own diplomatic representation. We must struggle to change our position from that of a free State to a completely independent State on the principle of " the right of nations to self-determination "; this means that we have the right to adhere to the French Union *of our own free will* (if

France remains a progressive country) or to withdraw from it if need be.

b) *UNIFICATION :* Viet Nam must be one, and its territorial integrity must be guaranteed. To achieve this, we must wreck the reactionary French colonialists' plot to partition our territory and to form what they impudently call the : "Nam Ky state", "Moi state",[26] "Thai state", "Nung state", etc. There could not be set up in our country three states differing from one another in their political, economic and cultural regimes. There is all the less reason, why there should exist in our country a free state North of the sixteenth parallel and an autonomous one in the South. Viet Nam must be worthy of the name *nation ;* that is to say, it is one and indivisible because Viet Nam is a *territorial, political, economic and cultural unity; this unity is not a fortuitous or a temporary combination, but one which, in the course of various historic epochs, has been built up by the sweat and toil of our people.*

c) *DEMOCRACY :* In maintaining and developing the democratic republican regime, strengthening the people's power and building the new democratic constitution, we must guard against changing our constitution into a meaningless and out-of-date one, along the lines of the bourgeois constitution. We must furthermore oppose all tendencies to sap the regime of popular representation, a progressive and adequate regime worthy of its birthright won by the people's revolutionary initiative in the course of their struggle for liberation. The country must always have a constitutional government which is elected, supported and controlled by the people.

[26] The author refers to the ethnic minority areas that the French sought to establish belatedly to form member states of an Indochinese Federation, thus diminishing the importance of Communist-dominated northern Viet-Nam. For obvious reasons, the Viet-Minh refused to accept such a solution. One indirect cause of the eventual outbreak of the Indochina War was the creation by the French of an "autonomous" Cochinchinese Republic in South Viet-Nam.

We must reorganize the administrative services, eliminate the reactionary and corrupt elements from the administrative offices as well as from the public services, and wipe out bureaucracy. We should do our utmost to transform Viet Nam into a really democratic country in the Far-East, worthy of ranking among the new democracies which have just been liberated from the fascist yoke.

d) *RENAISSANCE :* We must build up and consolidate the bases of the democratic regime by economic and cultural restoration and by national reform in material and spiritual fields.

On the one hand, we must produce and reproduce without interruption. We must push forward industrial, agricultural and cultural production to make good the war wounds so as to put an end to all signs of misery, corruption and devastation caused by eighty years of slavery. Everyone should make a contribution to the national restoration : the rich should put their capital into the enterprises, the able-bodied should work hard, those who have political and intellectual abilities should put all their initiative into drawing up plans and policies. We must respect labour, encourage private enterprises, reward those who have made sacrifices and punish all speculators and saboteurs. It is not enough simply to make Viet Nam a democratic state ; we must change it into a country with a progressive and independent economy.

On the other hand, we should meet the people's material needs, especially those of the working people (both manual and intellectual), so that they will have the necessary strength to produce ; we should strive to protect our race from physical degeneration, to reduce infant mortality and fight against all diseases.

Resistance war and national reconstruction

The resistance war consists of struggling for national unification and independence and repulsing the French colonialist attack. National reconstruction aims at establishing and consolidating the democratic republican regime, restoring and transforming the country. Like China, which struggled for many years against the Japanese, for a year now our people have been waging the resistance war and at the same time have been carrying out national reconstruction. That is an inherent characteristic of the struggle for the liberation of our country, one part of which is liberated and the other still oppressed by the imperialists.

In the reconstruction work, for a year now our people have striven to increase production, simultaneously supply the front and fight against famine, and repair roads, bridges, dykes, etc. This year, our people have won victories over three big enemies: famine, illiteracy and floods. Those are our tangible achievements. But we still lack a general plan for all our reconstruction work. The following examples are enough to prove that:

Putting into effect the slogan "not an inch of waste land", our compatriots in the mountain regions have in some places burnt down parts of the forest, clearing land for cultivation at random — a practice which is harmful to the preservation of forests and the prevention of floods.

In every province and locality, the slogan "increase production" is carried out without close guidance as to the nature of the crops, their quantity, time of growth and consumption, etc.

The efforts exerted by our people in a year are beyond imagination. However, one has the impression that they have thrown themselves into production like a wood-cutter who chops wood with his eyes shut — vigorously, but with much wasted effort.

It is time to work out an overall reconstruction plan for the whole country, to readjust every branch of production and to give rational guidance to national reform work.

Of course this work of planning will meet with difficulties because the situation has not yet been stabilized and the question of French interests in Indo-China has not yet been settled. Nevertheless, it is not absolutely impossible to draw up a preliminary plan on simple and realistic lines.

If we strive only for national reconstruction but neglect to struggle for sovereignty and territorial integrity, national independence will certainly not be recognized and our country will be reduced to an autonomous state. Our people are not a warlike people. In keeping with our people's deep love for peace, our government signed the Preliminary Agreement of March 6, 1946. But the treacherous behaviour of the French colonialists forced us to pursue the Resistance war to defend ourselves. We are ready to accept *an honourable armistice*, but as long as the French forces continue to attack and terrorize us, we must remain armed to defend ourselves until they recognize the impossibility of establishing again their domination over our country and of partitioning our territory. Has the Resistance war in the South only a local and provisional character or will it be transformed into a long-term Resistance? That is for the French to answer. As for us, we must thoroughly support the struggle of the people in the South in every field and we will increase our forces everywhere so as to be ready to face any eventuality and fight to the end.

Great Unity : a key task

To carry out Resistance and national reconstruction, we must mobilize all the forces of our country, fight against the French colonialists' policy of division, consolidate our ranks inside the country and win new support from outside.

That is why the internal unity of the whole people must be consolidated.

The policy of *great unity* advocated by President Ho Chi Minh must be carried out thoroughly and broadly.

Unity between nationalities : To frustrate the colonialist schemes to dupe the national minorities into opposing the majority people.

Unity between religions. To fight against the colonialist plot to make Catholic, Hoa Hao and Cao Dai compatriots oppose their own people.

National unity : To smash the colonialist scheme to make our compatriots in the South fight against those in the Centre and the North.

Unity between all different strata of the people: Side by side they must struggle against the common enemy to gain national independence.

Unity between all parties: All patriotic and democratic parties must put aside all prejudices so as to struggle hand in hand against the French reactionaries, the Vietnamese traitors and their organisations.

The entire people should unite into *a National Front to fight the reactionary French colonialists and wrest back complete independence.* For a year, nothing has been able to shake that Front, cemented by the blood of our fighters coming from the four corners of the country to defend the South. On that front, the whole people should act as one to fight the aggressors, repress the traitors, defend the Democratic Republican regime and reform our country — in short, to change Viet Nam into an independent, unified, free and happy country.

That is the objective aimed at by the *Viet Nam National League.* That Front represents an adequate form of national unity which our people have achieved in the struggle against the French reactionaries and the Vietnamese traitors. It must be broadened to include all parties and sects which are for national independence and democracy, as well as all patriotic non-party elements.

It might be asked : Is the league of the Vietnamese people only a political manœuvre being used to temporarily neutralize other political parties ? Certainly not ! It must be a lasting organisation able to mobilize all the broad masses to fulfil the tasks of national salvation and national reconstruction. It should never be regarded as a temporary and insignificant form of alliance between the parties.

But to broaden and consolidate the Viet Nam National League, we ought to develop and strengthen the *Viet Minh Front*, because the Viet Minh Front with its strong organizations naturally constitutes a firm basis for the National League. And to develop and consolidate the Viet Minh Front, it is necessary to unite and develop all organisations of the vanguard class, the Vietnamese working class. The alliance between workers, peasants and intellectuals must be especially firm.

Inside, our compatriots must closely, broadly and effectively unite. But that national unity alone is not enough. We must also unite with the allies outside our country. First we must unite with the French people who have made many sacrifices in their struggle for liberty and the just cause, and who with us, have a common enemy, the French reactionaries, the greedy monopolies and their lackeys, the reactionary colonialists. We have agreed to take part in the French Union but this Union must be a " democratic and fraternal union between free and equal people ", to use the words of Comrade Lozeray, member of the Central Committee of the French Communist Party at a session of the French Constituent Assembly on March 20, 1946. That Union should not be used as a cage to imprison the colonial peoples after "clipping their wings ". In our struggle to demand from France the respect of our sovereignty and territorial integrity, we must achieve unity of action with the French people and with all organizations faithful to the ideals of the French Revolution : liberty, equality, fraternity. For that reason we warmly hail the formation of the " Franco-Vietnamese Association " and we hope that it will become a steady bridge between the two peoples who are linked to one another by the same ideal.

We should ally ourselves not only with the French people, but also with all peace-loving and democratic peoples, particularly with the Chinese people, our great neighbours who are resolutely struggling for democracy, unification and independence. In a word, we must unite with all the oppressed peoples who are fighting to liberate themselves. During the second world war, we joined our efforts to those of the forces of counter-oppression in order to defeat the fascists. Today, the war is over but we must continue to stand side by side with the progressive forces to fight against the remnants of fascism and the international reactionaries to build democracy and world peace and to smash the schemes to draw mankind into an atrocious atomic third world war.

For that reason, our people must claim their place in the United Nations Organisation and in the international arena, as a people who have participated in the struggle against aggressive fascism, wrested power from the Japanese fascists, and now continue to struggle to exact from the French colonialists the respect of the Charter of the United Nations Organisation which was supported in San Francisco by France itself.

Wiping out errors

To fulfil these tasks, the entire people, and particularly the communists and the revolutionary fighters,
must correct their shortcomings and reject what is
wrong. President Ho Chi Minh often says: *"We
don't fear the enemy; we only fear the errors of our
comrades!"*

Indeed, has not the enemy attacked us successfully by exploiting our inadequacies, shortcomings and
errors ? That is why we must with determination eliminate all erroneous tendencies.

We should wipe out the *tendencies to anarchy and
indiscipline* seen in carelessness and disobedience to
orders from superiors, as well as infringements of
government instructions and of Party discipline : tendencies showing a misunderstanding of the democratic
regime. There are some who do not clearly realize the
meaning of democratic order and discipline ; they
think that a democratic regime can connive at disorder,
confusion and heedlessness. From this anarchy and
indiscipline will emerge, on the one hand, regionalism,
regional autonomism, on the other, corruption, abuse,
militarism and bureaucracy.

We must :

Root out the *tendencies to isolation and narrow-
mindedness* which are seen in the abuse of cadres'
abilities and in a wrong attitude towards certain events
as in carrying out the policy of national unity outlined
by the Party and President Ho Chi Minh. This harmful
tendency comes from the fear of the masses and from
a lack of confidence in the masses and in oneself; at

the same time it shows a mechanical interpretation of Marxist-Leninist theories expressed in abstract clichés repeated parrot-fashion.

Eliminate *subjectivity and " leftist " tendencies* which lead to acting even in unfavourable conditions ; to believing that one's personal desires are those of the masses ; to travelling " post-haste " without paying attention to the objective conditions of the situation and the real possibilities of the movement.

Eradicate *conservative and rightist tendencies* which lead us to cling to routine and to be hampered by the old formulas, to stick stubbornly to the old prejudices, to fail to recognize new changes early enough, to act with determination, the only spirit in conformity with our revolutionary era.

Eliminate the *tendency to compromise* beyond all principles with either the reactionaries or the companions in struggle. This tendency demonstrates a lack of determination in keeping firmly to one's position, an overestimation of the enemy and an underestimation of the strength of the masses, a failure to rely upon the masses or to use them as a strong rear guard. This tendency also demonstrates a wrong understanding of the National Front, and the existence of the belief that because we are in the same front we must always excuse one another, not criticising each other even moderately and with the support of evidence ! Like tendencies to isolation and narrow-mindedness, this tendency comes from a " lame policy " which doesn't take into account that criticism without solidarity is bad, but solidarity without criticism is worse.

Reject the *tendency to complacency*, being satisfied with one's small success ; that makes us become short-sighted, lessens our vigilance, weakens our spirit of criticism and self-criticism and creates the conception that the revolution is infallible, a detestable and dangerous conception which hinders our progress and keeps us away from the masses.

Wipe out the *tendency to pessimism* which makes us grumble and lack courage when facing the smallest obstacles, or makes us doubt and lose our heads at the least defeat, and consequently leads to worthless criticism or makes us give up the struggle and run away from our responsibility.

Those shortcomings and errors are the most widespread today among the people, cadres and the as yet unorganized masses, as in organizations, and in political, administrative, military and technical offices, etc. If we do not correct those errors in time, we cannot hope to realize true national unity to build up an *independent, united, democratic and prosperous country*.

Why do the above-mentioned shortcomings and errors exist ? In our opinion, due to the four following causes :

1 — The greater part of our economy comes from agriculture and handicrafts. The technical level of our people is low, and as a result, they lack generally a sense of organization. Our work is still routine, non-scientific and without perspective.

2 — Ours is a country of small production. Although led by the proletariat, the movement for the liberation

of our country possesses many petty - bourgeois characteristics such as wavering, lack of determination, hesistancy, lack of thoroughness. These defects are still numerous in our movement.

3 — For a long time our compatriots have not only been oppressed and exploited, but have also suffered from the obscurantist policy; they have never participated broadly in political and cultural activities, therefore their limited knowledge has a bad influence on the work of national salvation and of national reconstruction.

4 — The August Revolution was not carried out with sufficient determination and was therefore not strong enough to wipe out all rottenness of the outmoded regime. Many evil practices of that corrupt regime still persist and do harm to the new regime.

Our shortcomings and errors arise out of the concrete conditions of the Vietnamese revolutionary movement in its present stage.

However we are convinced that under the clearsighted leadership of President Ho Chi Minh and thanks to our people's march towards progress, we will effectively remedy those errors and shortcomings.

We should not delude ourselves into thinking that in a short time the Revolution can wipe out all the bad habits and customs of the old regime, which have become deeply rooted in our thoughts. Along with the political revolution, the cultural revolution with its " New life " movement must achieve the reformation of thoughts and customs, and the economic revolution should improve the people's living standards.

so as to create favourable conditions for the success of the political and cultural revolution which is in full swing. But if we are determined to fight those bad tendencies by all means, it will be possible to correct them rapidly, provided every citizen and every revolutionary combatant sincerely exercises criticism and self-criticism and clearly understands his duty to exterminate all these evil tendencies.

Training of cadres

After settling the question of the political line to be followed and the tasks to be fulfilled, the question of cadres proves to be the most important one to solve.

Who applies the political line and carries out the tasks? Of course it is the whole people, but first of all it is the cadres, who are the vanguard elements devoting themselves actively to the work of propaganda and organization, who devote themselves to leading the masses to carry out the policies of the Government and the Party, and to serving as good examples for the people.

We must admit that one of the shortcomings of our present movement lies in the lack of cadres. Few cadres for much work, hence the weakness of one person having too many irons in the fire. Many cadres are unable to accomplish their tasks or to complete them thoroughly, or they work thoughtlessly in a slap-dash manner without any pre-established plan, or display a narrow minded approach to their work.

Therefore, a decisive task in this present hour is to strive to have a greater number of cadres, and to have good cadres ; to promote existing cadres in a rational and just way and to train new ones patiently and methodically. Every cadre must guide the novices who work side by side with him so as to create new cadres. So many active workers and peasants, so many youths fully devoted to the Revolution are ready to accept all sacrifices! Have confidence in them, employ them boldly, guide them patiently, *but do not forget to control them*.

At present, we are overwhelmed with work. It is necessary to mobilize all manpower and wealth. No ability, no effort must be wasted. Affairs of State are not the monopoly of some special group of persons, some party or some revolutionary class, but they are the common business of the whole people. Naturally the choice of cadres must not be prompted by personal feelings, but we must not either be too rigorous in the selection of new recruits, as the case is for some comrades at present.

There are not enough of the schools founded by the Government to ensure the training of new administrative, judicial, military and technical cadres. In addition to these, the revolutionary organization must frequently open political training courses and organize talks and lectures to which the public will be widely admitted.

Simultaneously with the extension of mass education and the struggle against illiteracy, the development of higher education is greatly needed as well as a revision of the curriculum, and the selection of students to be sent abroad.

At the present time the question of cadres is a contradictory one. The great majority of cadres, schooled by the revolutionary struggle, are loyal, eager and skilful elements with a good political background, and a fair degree of organization, but most of them have a poor educational level (the fault is not theirs, for being in the majority born of the labouring masses, they have remained illiterate or have not been able to complete their schooling). On the other hand, the technicians and intellectuals who formerly graduated from the French Universities have a certain cultural level but know little about politics. (We cannot reproach them with this either, for throughout our eighty years of slavery, have the imperialists ever thought of educating the Vietnamese people politically? Have they ever allowed the Vietnamese people to study or go in for politics ? Their sole concern was the formation of a class of young Vietnamese intellectuals who would serve them merely as their tools...)

Therefore the training of existing cadres as well as of new ones at this present time must aim at suppressing this contradiction. Existing cadres must be granted time and material conditions in which to raise their educational level and theoretical political knowledge. A movement to stimulate a fervent eagerness for study, without causing any neglect of the daily task, but co-ordinated with this task, must be launched. By our propaganda, we must encourage the intellectuals and technicians to join political groups and attend political training classes.

We must criticize the wrong attitude of some Viet Minh cadres (including communists) who make light of intellectuals and technicians, are prejudiced against them, keep no contact with them, do not employ them and are adverse to learning from them. But at the same time we must put right the point of view of some non - Viet Minh intellectuals who think that the Viet Minh and communist cadres who have worthily' led the Revolution to the seizure of power must now " withdraw " from the political arena and transfer the task of national reconstruction to trained intellectuals and technicians.

Those who nurture these thoughts fail to understand that the communist and Viet Minh militants who marched in the vanguard during the period of underground struggle for the liberation of the Fatherland must now more than ever keep their vanguard role, devoting their political knowledge and revolutionary spirit to the work of national defence and national reconstruction.

A comforting knowledge for us is the fact that, from the August Revolution onwards, intellectuals have adhered in ever greater numbers to the Viet Minh League. Struggling among the people's ranks, they have shown an eager patriotism and respect for Party discipline. They are now developing into good revolutionary cadres, greatly deserving the confidence of the entire people.

CONCLUSION

August 1945,

August 1946.

One year has passed, worth a whole decade for the experiences gained. By the August Revolution, the Vietnamese people have broken the imperialist fetters, to march forward with giant strides. Steeled through their thousand years' history of struggle and sacrifice, the Vietnamese people are enthusiastically launched upon the winning of a bright future. They have always been a young, healthy people whose rich and powerful vitality continues to develop with every passing day, to the astonishment of the whole world.

The Vietnamese people have covered quite a good distance on their path of independence and liberation. However, the goal has not yet been reached. They have to press forward and continue to press forward. Many obstacles have arisen on the road already travelled, but thanks to their *spirit of unity, to their struggle and their strenuous efforts*, the Vietnamese people have gained their first victories.

In these days, the resistance in South Viet Nam and South-Central Viet Nam is still going on. This heroic, tenacious struggle for self-defence develops the achievements of the August Revolution and further steels the traditional virtues of our people.

The French reactionary colonialists hoped to solve the Vietnamese problem by armed force according to their own will. But the Resistance war carried out by the Vietnamese people has shattered their illusions. The Vietnamese people are ready to wage a long struggle to overcome all difficulties and obstacles and resolutely fight all brutal plunderers and their stooges until they recover the integrity of their territory and gain complete INDEPENDENCE, FREEDOM and HAPPINESS.

THE
RESISTANCE
WILL WIN

by

TRUONG CHINH

[FACSIMILE EDITION]

HANOI

FOREIGN LANGUAGES PUBLISHING HOUSE

1960

CONTENTS

We are happy to present to our readers the English translation of " The Resistance Will Win ".

In the light of Marxism — Leninism, Truong Chinh, a revolutionary militant from his earliest days and one of the leaders of the August Revolution, wrote this book after the hostilities in Viet Nam had become nation-wide, and at a time when the prospect of final victory was far form clear in everyone's mind.

The course of events confirmed this clear analysis, which gave a decisive orientation to the Vietnamese Resistance war and served as a guide to the entire people in their fight, under the leadership of the Party, against colonialism and for freedom and national independence.

PREFACE

The soil of Viet Nam is being trampled by a foul and savage enemy. The Vietnamese people are waging an heroic resistance war ; they are determined to avenge themselves in blood. Will Viet Nam disappear or survive ? Will the Vietnamese people succeed or fail ? These are the questions being asked by our compatriots and by many people in other countries.

Here is our answer : the Vietnamese people cannot be reduced to bondage ! This is so because the movement for the liberation of Viet Nam is an integral part of the new democratic movement which is rising throughout the world. As for the enemies of Viet Nam, the French colonialists, they are part of out-of-date, decadent imperialism, which has been condemned by history.

At present, the Vietnamese armed forces are still weaker than those of the enemy ; therefore it is necessary to prolong the Resistance war. In the course of the fighting we shall develop our forces, gradually wearing down the enemy's strength, awaiting the day when we can crush him completely. This Resistance war must be waged by the entire people in every field — military, political, economic and cultural — so that, wherever the enemy goes, he meets our fierce resistance, which encircles and chokes him, making it impossible for him to live in peace in our country.

This book sets forth the guiding principles of the fight to the death against the reactionary French colonialists for the genuine independence and reunification of the Fatherland, for the maintenance and development of the democratic republican regime of Viet Nam, and for the small contribution that the Vietnamese people can make to the safeguarding of world peace and democracy.

Viet Nam's armed resistance is a just war. A just war generally receives much support and derives immense strength from the people. However, the experiences of the Abyssinian people in the struggle against the Italian fascists in 1935-1936 have shown that even a just war may be doomed to failure if the military command commits blunders, if propaganda, mobilization and foreign policy are weak. We must profit from this lesson.

To win final victory in this long and hard struggle is not an easy task. Success can only be achieved on the following fundamental conditions : the correctness of our political line, the achievement of close national unity, the consolidation of our rear, the heroism of our army and people and the competence of our command.

This Resistance war enhances the Vietnamese people's prestige throughout the world and develops the best traditions of the descendants of Lac-Hong. All our compatriots have heard the sacred call of their Fatherland, and are rising up in response. Determined to fulfil their duty to the Fatherland, they set one another examples of how to struggle. of how to show themselves worthy of their ancestors.

The noteworthy strong point of the resistance under the Trân dynasty consisted of clever stratagems and ruses.

The noteworthy strong point of the resistance in the reign of the Later Lês was perserverance and endurance.

The noteworthy strong point of the resistance during the reign of Quang Trung lay in speed and ferocity in attack. [27]

Under the leadership of President Ho Chi Minh, our national hero, a synthesis of the historical experiences of Viet Nam and other countries is being achieved in order to turn defeat into victory. Big sacrifices and strenuous efforts are being made by the entire people in all parts of our country.

However savage and evil the reactionary French colonialists may be, the long resistance of our people will certainly be victorious.

The Resistance will win, *such is our unshakable faith. Such also is the title which we have given to this book, which comprises articles dealing with the Resistance, published in Nos. 70 to 81 * of the review* Su that **, *and later revised and amended. The book is published by the Su That Publishing House on the occasion of the second anniversary of the outbreak of the Resistance war in south Viet Nam.*

North Viet Nam, September 19 1947
TRUONG CHINH

---

* Issues from March 4, 1947 to August 1, 1947
**·*Truth.*

[27] Truong Chinh refers here to mythical and historical heroes of Viet-Nam's past.

WHOM ARE WE FIGHTING ?

The Vietnamese people are waging a sacred war to win freedom and independence, to defend the territory handed down to them by their ancestors. The whole country is rising against the enemy.

Who is the enemy ? The enemy is the reactionary French colonialists, who are using force to re-invade our country.

The reactionary French colonialists are our deadly foes, our main enemy. They are the enemy to be damned forever, the enemy whose advance we must make speed to check. They are the enemy to be crushed and annihilated.

We are not fighting against France, because France is a democratic country which, in its new constitution, states that France will " never launch any aggressive war and never use force to infringe upon the liberty of any people ".

Are we fighting against the French people ? No ! Because the French people, who love " liberty, equality, fraternity ", have no desire to invade our country. Because they know that, in this aggression, their children will die on the battlefield, and that only a handful of greedy capitalists will benefit from it. The more we fight, the more the French people will hate the French colonialists ; they will demand an armistice from the French Government, and the withdrawal from Indochina of the French reactionaries who oppose their aspirations and bring dishonour upon the name of the new France.

Naturally we are not fighting against the French people ; we are not even fighting against all types of French colonialists.

President Ho Chi Minh has said : " *There are French businessmen who want to carry on their business activities in Viet Nam. They know that to conduct business and make profits, they must sincerely cooperate with the Vietnamese people. They know that in order to be able to provide that cooperation, Viet Nam must be independent and unified. These are the non-reactionary colonialists. As for those who scheme or use force to subjugate our people, they are the reactionary colonialists* ". *

We are only fighting against the French reactionaries who " scheme or use force to subdue us " and who refuse to recognize our right to independence and reunification. The more we fight, the more clearly will the relatively less reactionary colonialist elements realize that the aggressive

---

* Reply to journalists' questions, January 1, 1947.

war in Viet Nam is harmful. They will oppose the stubborn reactionary colonialists and advocate a peaceful settlement and co-operation with us in order to "conduct business and make profits" in our country.

Are we fighting all types of colonialists all over the world ? Of course not ! We are not so stupid as to declare war on those who remain neutral, who do not send troops against us, thus sowing needless hatred between them and ourselves.

In a word, we are neither Francophobe nor xenophobe. We are only against the reactionary French colonialists.

We pledge that we shall never allow these colonialists to place their yoke again upon our compatriots. We are rising up, arms in hand. We shall never lay down our arms so long as the reactionary French colonialists are not completely eliminated from our country.

The French soldiers, legionaries and colonial troops, are sent by force to Indochina to fight us. They are mere pitiful tools of the reactionary French colonialists. They are forced to leave their homes, their parents, their wives and children, and are sent here to serve as cannon fodder for the imperialists and colonialists.

We must fire on them because they are obliged to fire on us, in the interests of the reactionary French colonialists. In this war against the reactionary French colonialists, we cannot abstain from fighting the French and colonial soldiers. But, in truth, we do not hate them. On the contrary, we and they both have a common enemy, the reactionary French colonialists. When the French and colonial soldiers come to understand this, not only will they refuse to fire on us, but they will even come over to our side with their arms, and together with us they will turn their arms against the French reactionaries. That is why, while fighting the French reactionaries, we shall miss no opportunity to make progaganda among the French soldiers, legionaries and colonial troops, and shall treat them well when they are taken prisoner.

As for the puppet soldiers, they are our compatriots; most of them are peasants. The colonialists are making use of them to fight against the Fatherland. We must strive all the more vigorously to enlighten them in order to win them to join the ranks of the resistance with their arms, and, together with us, to annihilate the aggressors, in atonement for their offences against our compatriots.

If we succeed in achieving all this, the enemy ranks will disintegrate and the reactionary French colonialists will be isolated.

To isolate the enemy in order to overthrow him, that is the common tactic of a class or of a nation that is determined to fight and to win.

II

WHY MUST WE FIGHT ?

In the appeal to wage a war of resistance made to our compatriots on December 20, 1946 by President Ho Chi Minh, he said :

" Because we love peace, we made concessions ; yet the more concessions we made, the more the French colonialists exerted pressure on us, because they had decided to invade our country again ".

Indeed, we did make numerous concessions to the French colonialists. But, greedy and savage, they broke their word, trampling on loyalty and justice. They have attacked us, so we must fight back in self-defence.

In August 1945, the Japanese were defeated. Our people rose up to seize back power. On September 23,

1945, the French colonialists attacked and occupied Saigon, once again unleashing an aggressive war upon our country.

On March 6, 1946, the French colonialists signed a "Preliminary Agreement", after which we allowed French troops to enter the North and Centre of Viet Nam. But they did not implement the Agreement. Not only did they fail to effect the cessation of hostilities in south Viet Nam, but they established a puppet government in the form of the "Autonomous State of south Viet Nam", and attacked and occupied the South-West of Central Viet Nam with the intention of forming a "Western State". At the same time, they attacked Son La and Lai Chau in north Viet Nam, and occupied the regions of Lang Son and Hai Ninh, with the intention of forming a "Nung State". At the same time, they occupied the coast from Haiphong to Mong Cai to found a "Federal zone". *

---

* We quote some documents to prove the perfidious schemes of the French colonialists :

Immediately after the signing of the Preliminary Agreement of March 6, 1946, French troops came to north Viet Nam and the northern part of Central Viet Nam. General Leclerc, commander of French forces in the Far East, sent to the officers under his command the following directive :

"You have not only to restore the former French order, but you must also defend French interests during the negotiations being held in Indochina and Paris.

"These defensive measures will be realized either by moderate steps bringing continual progress day by day, *or by force* wherever *needed...*"

On April 18, 1946, General Valluy, French commander in Northern Indochina, sent to the officers under his command the following directive :

"In every garrison, immediately upon his arrival, the commander must draw up a basic security plan. This plan

On September 14, 1946, a *modus vivendi* was signed between France and Viet Nam. According to this *modus vivendi*, we recognized the cultural and economic interests of France in Viet Nam. As for France, she agreed to carry out the cease-fire, and to respect democratic freedoms in south Viet Nam.

Implementing the *modus vivendi*, we gave back to France the Pasteur Institute in Hanoi and ceased fire in south Viet Nam. On the other hand, France took advantage

---

must include permanent defence of the army's barracks, and provide especially for action to *occupy the town*, because generally the best means of defence is attack.

"The plan must have a threefold aim :

1 — "To isolate and occupy in a very short space of time the enemy's points of resistance, such as the principal streets inhabited by Vietnamese and Chinese residents, all barracks, unreliable localities, arms depots and military equipment stores ;

2 — To occupy all important points in the localities (public services, bridges, tactical points) ;

3 — By applying the above measures, to guarantee speedily the defence of the life and property of French residents of the localities concerned.

"When this plan has been accomplished in general, it must immediately be supplemented by methods having the effect of gradually modifying forms of action in order eventually to change from the stage of purely military activity to *the stage of coup d'état* "

As early as this therefore, the French colonialists had formed the intention to occupy our towns and overthrow our Government. On April 6, 1946, Valluy had sent secret directives to Colonel Vicaire, concerning the invasion of the Nung State. [28]

---

[28] The documents are quoted correctly but deliberately misinterpreted. Since the French had only 5,000 troops north of the 16th parallel at the time of the outbreak of hostilities, their intentions, as the third point of the cited document indicates, were defensive. The plan was in fact implemented after the outbreak of fighting in December, 1946; for several months, the French garrisons of Hanoi, Haiphong, Nam-Dinh, and Hué, among others, fought wholly cut off from each other. The Vinh garrison was overrun very early in the fighting.

of our sincerity to send troops everywhere into the countryside to arrest our patriots in south Viet Nam, and to re-establish the " Councils of Notables ", a French puppet administration in the villages. At the same time they blockaded the port of Haiphong, intending to seize control of our Customs, thus creating financial difficulties for our Government.

On November 20, 1946, they obstructed the collection of customs dues by our Government, and fired on our security and customs men while the latter were carrying out their duties. Our troops fired back in self-defence.[29] D'Argenlieu and Valluy ordered the outright occupation of Haiphong and Lang Son, simultaneously with the landing of thousands of French troops at Tourane, in violation of the agreements signed.

Thus, the French colonialists first violated the Preliminaly Agreement of March 6, 1946, and then the *modus vivendi* of September 14.

" Proceed to Cô Tô and prepare for an attack on the Nung State, around Mong cai.

" Leave a part of your troops in Cô Tô and Van Hoa and occupy these places until you receive fresh orders. "

On April 21, 1946, referring to General Valluy's directive, Colonel Vicaire reported to his commander on the occupation of the Nung State :

" Our action may be defined as the occupation of the base of a triangle : Hanoi — Hai Duong — Hongay, Mong Cai, the apex of which is Lang Son. "

On the same day, reporting on the action of Gribelin's troops in making use of bandits to sow troubles in Quang Yen region, to prepare for the occupation by French troops of the mining area, Vicaire again wrote :

[29] This is a quite accurate and restrained account—a great deal more restrained than some Western versions. In reality, the French challenged a Chinese junk carrying gasoline for the Viet-Minh forces, whereupon the latter erected street barricades throughout Haiphong. A French bulldozer sent to demolish the barricades was fired upon. A French cruiser, mistaking a fleeing crowd on the edge of the city for attacking Viet-Minh, opened fire. In the ensuing panic, nearly 6,000 persons were killed.

No further doubt about their intentions was possible

The French reactionaries' scheme to re-invade our country became obvious.

But that was not all. Following the Haiphong and Lang Son incidents, the French colonialists staged repeated provocations in every spot in which they were established.

Their actions poured oil on the flames. The situation was very tense.

Our people no longer trusted the word of the French, so they prepared for any eventuality. Earthen barricades, fortifications and trenches appeared in Hanoi and in the provinces where French troops were stationed.

On December 16, 1946, all the French colonialist ring-leaders in Indochina met in Haiphong. On the following day, French troops resorted to provocations and launched an attack in Hanoi. On December 17, 1946, the French troops crossed the barricade in Hang Bun Street, in the

---

" In the present circumstances, the occupation of the mining area of Mao Khê and Uông Bi by the regular army, as proposed by the Tonkin Coal-mining Company, seems impossible of accomplishment.

" However, simultaneously with the *occupation of the Nung State*, and the political activities which must be carried out behind the Hongay — Mong Cai coastal area, attention must also be given to the actions of a group of partisans. »

The above-mentioned proofs, which are but a few of many, are sufficient to expose the French colonialists' criminality. Faced with such clear proof, can the French invaders still deny that they attacked and occupied Viet Nam premeditatedly ?

Can their propaganda accusing Viet Nam of attacking them first have any validity ?

Yên Ninh quarter of Hanoi, and fired on the headquarters of the self-defence forces in that street. Their fire was returned. Then the French forces, armed with mortars, machine-guns, cannon and grenades, attacked the Yên Ninh quarters. They broke into houses, raped women, slaughtered children and pillaged property. They thus created a state of war in the heart of Hanoi. The reactionary French colonialists in Indochina were availing themselves of the Cabinet crisis in France — the Bidault Government had resigned, the Blum Government was not yet in power — to carry out a policy of *fait accompli*. From that time [30] onwards, there existed generalised war between the Vietnamese people and the French colonialists, a war provoked by the French colonialists.

On December 18, 1946, French forces occupied two Vietnamese public offices : the Ministry of Finance and the Ministry of Communications and Public Works. At the same time, Morlière, the butcher of Yên Ninh quarter, sent an ultimatum to our Government, demanding disarmament of the self-defence forces, and threatening to assume control of public security in Hanoi.

The French colonialists were pressing their plans hard. The atmosphere of hostility between Viet Nam and France became extremely tense. Then, on the night of December 19, 1946, under severe provocation on the part of French troops in Hanoi, fighting broke out in the capital and hostilities spread throughout Viet Nam.

Events have proved that those who failed to keep their word, and who broke the Preliminary Agreement of March 6 and the *modus vivendi* of September 14, are the reactionary French colonialists. Those who provoked war and attacked us throughout the country are the reactionary

---

[30] It is a documented fact that some of the French representatives in Indochina wished to see the negotiations fail. An appeal telegraphed by Premier Léon Blum to Ho Chi Minh in an attempt to head off the conflict was sidetracked in Saigon for four days and transmitted to Hanoi only after the fighting had broken out.

French colonialists. They used force to invade our country and to partition it. We could not continue to make further concessions to them. Had we done so, our Government would have become a puppet government, and our people would have been enslaved. For that reason, we were compelled to resist, to fight the reactionary French colonialists, in order to defend the integrity of our country and to maintain our sovereignty.

President Ho Chi Minh declared :

" Even if we must sacrifice everything, we are determined not to lose our country, not to live as slaves. "

(Appeal of December 20, 1946).

The French reactionaries try to make propaganda by saying that we attacked them first, on December 19. In truth, they are merely striving to conceal their own crimes : they attacked us as early as November 20, in Haiphong and Lang Son, and on December 17 in the capital ; they attacked us immediately after the signing of the Preliminary Agreement of March 6, 1946, and even before that again. They brazenly cry : " Viet Nam is acting in contravention of the agreements ". In this way, they hope to delude people and to make them forget the French violations of the agreements. But facts are stubborn things, and they must bear the full burden of responsibility in the eyes of history, in the eyes of the world and of the French people.

Honest people must today acknowledge that our people love peace and that our Government is moderate in the extreme. But if fight we must, we are determined to fight. Our long forbearance has kindled a deep hatred in our people's hearts, which will blaze forth with invincible power.

III

WHAT ARE WE FIGHTING FOR?

The reactionary French colonialists intend to use methods of attrition to grab our country. Furthermore, they are applying the policy of *fait accompli* to continue their reactionary manœuvres in Indochina, whatever the changes in the political situation in France may be.

If the French people ask questions, they will be told: "The matter has been settled, nothing has happened!"

To defeat the policy of "attrition" and *fait accompli* of the French colonialists, the Vietnamese people must fight!

France has signed an Agreement with Viet Nam. Why should those who call themselves representatives of France expect the Vietnamese people alone to implement the Agreement, while they themselves are free to trample on it?

How can the reactionary French colonialists, of whom d'Argenlieu and his clique are mere lackeys, dare to employ "ultimatums" with our Government ? To oppose the faith-less, unjust, insolent behaviour of the reactionary French colonialists, the Vietnamese people must fight !

For nearly a century, the French colonialists oppressed and exploited the Vietnamese people. During the five years of the Second World War, they opened the gates of Indochina to the Japanese fascists and, together with them, imposed untold hardships and burdens upon our people. Today, seeing us win power and a measure of freedom, they are concerned for their sordid interests. They look upon us with hatred. According to the *modus vivendi* of September 14, 1946, we recognized their cultural and economic in-terests (interests, alas, which they founded on our people's sweat and blood, but which they were incapable of protect-ing, letting them fall into Japanese hands ; it was our people and our people alone, who wrested them back with the August uprising !), but they were not satisfied. They want to make our people serve them again as soldiers and coolies, and to pay them taxes. They want to muzzle our people, torture, massacre and imprison them as before. To wipe out the cowardly, greedy French colonialists, the Vietnamese people must fight !

How much blood have our ancestors shed because of the French invaders ! Today we must again shed our blood because of them !

How many of the flower of our youth have been sacri-ficed on French scaffolds and in French prisons ? How many women have been violated, how many children burnt alive ? How many mothers have lost their little ones, brothers lost their sisters, husbands been torn from their wives ? How many houses have gone up in flames, villages fallen victim to terrorist raids ? How much gold and rice has been plundered ? How many churches and tombs have been desecrated, pagodas and temples burnt and razed ? To annihilate the French reactionaries, to defend themselves, to defend civilization and the cause of justice, the Vietnamese people must fight !

The guns fired in our resistance war spit the hatred of the Vietnamese people in the faces of the French reactionaries.

No ! The Vietnamese people do not only demand from the French colonialists that they respect agreements signed in due form and order ; they do not only demand reversion to the position as it was on November 20 and December 17, 1946, as some people have mistakenly understood.

No ! The shots now being fired are those of a long resistance ! We must win independence and national unification. Independence and unification within the French Union if need be, but it must be independence and unification ! To respect the Preliminary Agreement of March 6, 1946 and the *modus vivendi* of September 14, 1946 is to recognize immediately the complete independence and the complete unification of Viet Nam. Only on these conditions can peace be restored. Otherwise, the Vietnamese people can do nothing but fight, fight and fight again — fight until they achieve the complete annihilation of all the rapacious reactionaries on their beloved soil.

The French reactionaries are attempting to set up a puppet government for the whole country. Then they will proclaim the recognition of the fake independence and unification of a Viet Nam headed by that Government. But their treacherous schemes are doomed to failure. The Vietnamese people are not so easily deceived as they think.[31]

Some of us say that the slogan " independance and unification within the French Union " implies a contradiction. Why does Viet Nam agree to remain part of the French Union when it claims to be independent ? These friends forget that the Vietnamese people have firm confidence in themselves and trust the French people ; therefore they do not fear to remain part of the French Union. The Vietnamese people are ready to co-operate with France, because they know that such co-operation, if it is sincere and based on equality and free consent, will be beneficial to both sides in the present international imbroglio. The Vietnamese people do not want the French people and the democratic world to misunderstand, to think that Viet Nam wishes to leave the French Union in order to join some reactionary bloc hostile to the forces of peace and democracy...

There are others who say : the slogan " independence and unification within the French Union " betrays a lack of firmness in resistance and hopes for peaceful negotiation with France. We reply : The Vietnamese people do not hate the French people, nor are we fighting against them ; so why should we not be on friendly terms with them ? However the Vietnamese people know that in order to establish friendly relations with the French people, they must resolutely break down the wall which separates the French and the Vietnamese peoples — that wall is the French colonialists. We are determined to annihilate the French reactionaries, who daily widen the gulf which

[31] This was a completely accurate forecast of the turn of events. Emperor Bao-Dai was persuaded in 1948 by the French to head an anti-Communist Vietnamese regime. It never acquired the popularity necessary to become a serious rival to Ho Chi Minh's government.

separates the two peoples, both of whom love peace, justice and freedom.

To achieve the above-mentioned political aim of the resistance war (independence and unification within the French Union), mere diplomacy with France is ineffective. We must wage a resistance war, we must take military action. Here are the military aims of our resistance war :

1 — To annihilate the enemy forces in our country,

2 — To take back the whole country,

3 — To crush completely the aggressive designs of the enemy.

Our people advocate a long resistance ; this means to strive to achieve military aims in order to realize our political aims. If France recognizes the " independence and unification of Viet Nam within the French Union ", we shall agree ; otherwise, when the resistance of Viet Nam has scored final victory, Viet Nam will become an independent state outside the framework of the French Union.

IV

THE CHARACTER OF OUR RESISTANCE

In history, there are two kinds of wars : just wars and unjust wars. Just wars are wars against oppressors and conquerors to safeguard the freedom and independence of the peoples. Unjust wars are wars aimed at the seizure of territories, at usurption of the freedom and happiness of the majority of the people of such territories.

Our people are fighting the reactionary French colonialists in order to regain freedom and independence, to defend and liberate themselves ; therefore, our resistance war is a revolutionary war, a people's war of self-defence, a just and progressive war. On the other hand, the French colonialists are invading our country with the aim of oppressing and exploiting our people as before ; therefore, the aggressive war of the French colonialists is an unjust and reactionary war . . .

A just war always enjoys warm support from people of goodwill, and from progressive nations all over the world. Sound public opinion and the peace-loving peoples always spurn and hold in contempt an unjust war.

We are not surprised that, so far, world opinion has not supported France, but that on the contrary, many countries (especially India, Burma, Indonesia and Malaya) uphold and encourage us.

This is one of the many factors which weaken the morale of the French soldiers and strengthen the determination of our army.

On the other hand, although the August Revolution won power for the Vietnamese people, it did not completely liberate the whole country. The present resistance war will fulfil the task of national liberation.

Though the August Revolution set up the regime of the Democratic Republic of Viet Nam, this regime is not yet perfect. The present resistance war will extend and consolidate the democratic republican regime of Viet Nam and develop it on the basis of new democracy.

That is why Viet Nam's armed resistance has not only the character of national liberation, but also that of new democracy. Is it not part of the great democratic movement now blazing forth throughout the world ?

Carrying on the work of the August Revolution, this resistance is a revolutionary war with the character of national independence, democracy and freedom. *In the crucible of the resistance, a new Viet Nam is being forged : an independent, unified, democratic, prosperous Viet Nam — a new democratic Viet Nam.*

There are some friends who think that if our presen struggle has a national and democratic character, while the colonialists are being fought, land must at the same time be taken from the landlords and distributed to the tillers. We say to them : This resistance war is fulfilling the task of national liberation and is developing new democracy. At present, we shall limit ourselves to the confiscation of land and other property belonging to Vietnamese traitors in order on the one hand, to distribute this land to the peasants, and, on the other, swell the budget of the resistance. This does not mean that we shall absolutely not carry out land reform during the course of the resistance war. But it must be undertaken step by step, in such a way as to differentiate among the feudalists, and isolate the French colonialist aggressors.

This resistance war is a *people's war*. The overwhelming majority of our people are peasants. Nearly all the fighters of our regular, militia and guerilla forces are also peasants. Our resistance is in fact a *peasant war led by the working class*.

The Vietnamese people are not struggling for themselves alone. They are struggling for their own liberation and at the same time for the defence of world peace. The French reactionaries who are invading Viet Nam are part and parcel of international reaction. Their ranks consist of big French financiers and French fascists who collaborated with the nazis. Their army consists of a great number of German soldiers who were formerly members of Hitler's fascist armies. A number of French colonialists who took part in the resistance to the German fascists during the last world war, such as Valluy, Morliere, etc., today, because of their seifish and shameful interests, have betrayed the ideal of opposition to aggression. They are collaborating with the magnates of French capital and have become their lackeys in the aggression against Viet Nam.

That is why, when the Vietnamese people fight the reactionary French colonialists, they are fighting against the remnants of the fascist forces, sworn enemies of world peace, who openly violate the United Nations and Atlantic Charters. The Vietnamese people realize that only when the reactionary French colonialists have been wiped out of Viet Nam, will the French and Vietnamese peoples, both loving independence and peace, be able genuinely to co-operate within the French Union, and in the great democratic family of the world.

Thus, the resistance in Viet Nam is a progressive war in which we are fighting for *freedom, independence, democracy and peace.*

V

RESISTANCE IN THE MILITARY FIELD[32]

Many people think that resistance consists only in sending troops to the front fight the enemy. In fact, to take up arms and kill the enemy represents only one aspect of the problem. The resistance of our people must be carried out in every field : military, economic, political and cultural.

In the military field, how must we fight ?

Resistance in the military field means using every measure, every stratagem, to maintain and develop our own forces, while destroying those of the enemy. It means using force to drive the invader out of our country.

The guiding principle of the strategy of our whole resistance must be to prolong the war.

[32] Chapter V as a whole constitutes one of the clearest statements made by a Communist leader in the field of revolutionary war and deserves particularly careful reading in view of its present application in South Viet-Nam.

To protract the war is the key to victory. Why must the war be protracted ? Because if we compare our forces with those of the enemy, it is obvious that the enemy is still strong, and we are still weak. The enemy's country is an industrial one — ours is an agricultural country. The enemy has planes, tanks, warships ; as for us, we have only rudimentary weapons. The enemy troops are well-trained, ours are not inured to war. If we throw the whole of our forces into a few battles to try and decide the outcome, we shall certainly be defeated and the enemy will win. On the other hand, if while fighting we maintain our forces, expand them, train our army and people, learn military tactics, strive to secure in sufficient quantities the things of which we are short, strengthen our weak points and at the same time wear down the enemy forces, we shall weary and discourage them in such a way that, strong as they are, they will become weak and will meet defeat instead of victory. In short, if we prolong the war, thanks to our efforts, our forces will grow stronger, the enemy forces will be weakened, their already low morale will become still lower, their already poor finances will become still poorer. The more we fight, the more united our people at home will be, and the more the world democratic movement will support us from outside. On the other hand, the more the enemy fights, the more the anti-war and democratic movement in France will check his hands ; the revolutionary movement in the French colonies will oblige the enemy to divide his forces ; and he will find himself in a position of isolation in the international arena. To achieve all these results, the war must be prolonged, and we must have time. Time works for us — time will be our best strategist, if we are determined to pursue the resistance war to the end.

Under the Trân dynasty, our people waged resistance three times in 31 years to defeat the Mongol invaders. Under the Later Lê dynasty, it took us ten years of resistance to wipe out the cruel Ming troops. The Chinese people carried out resistance for eight years to free themselves from Japanese occupation. The lesson of those long resistance wars is very clear. Those who want " lightning war and rapid victory ", who want to bring the whole of our forces to the battle-front to win speedy victory and rapidly to decide the outcome of the war, do not profit from the invaluable experiences of history ; indeed, they understand nothing of the strategy necessary to our people in this resistance war. They do not believe in the power of the masses for resistance. All that they would achieve would be the premature sacrifice of the bulk of our forces in a few adventurous battles ; they would commit heroic but useless suicide. They pretend to underestimate the enemy. Yet they are the very ones who are afraid of the enemy and of a long resistance war.

What is our line in the fighting? It is to attack actively, and rapidly to decide every battle.

We are attacked. The enemy is stronger than we are. If we only remain on the defensive, only defend ourselves where we are attacked, the more we fight the weaker we shall become — the more we fight the more we shall be defeated. Therefore, in every campaign and battle, the weak points of the enemy must be discovered and attacked, and we must attack actively to annihilate his forces. If we attack, we must do it quickly and decide the battle rapidly. (From the strategic viewpoint, we must prolong the war ; but in every individual campaign and from a tactical viewpoint, we must achieve rapid settlements.) It is only by applying the tactics of quick attack that we can destroy the enemy sector by sector. The upshot of many battles in which the enemy is destroyed sector by sector, will be to weaken his forces as a whole, to demoralize them. Our forces, on the other hand, will increase and our fighters' morale will be enhanced. We shall go on in this way until we reach the point at which we are sufficiently strong to launch a general counter-offensive to defeat the enemy on all battle-fronts and to recover the whole of our territory.

To attack actively and to stamp out the enemy in every battle we must constantly apply mobile tactics, advancing as deeply as possible, withdrawing as far as possible. We must concentrate our forces rapidly, launch lightning attacks, then disperse with agility. In other words, from a tactical viewpoint, we must wage guerilla and mobile warfare.

Guerilla warfare is the method of fighting in partisan units or with relatively small groups of the regular army disguised as civilians and mingling with the people. Though these forces are armed only with rudimentary weapons, they are extremely active. They attack the enemy from behind, outflank him or launch sudden attacks on his weak points. They pretend to attack the enemy's right flank while actually attacking his left, they concentrate for attack and disperse to dodge the enemy's reply. They cut communication lines, harass the enemy while he is eating or sleeping, wear out his strength, cause him weariness and distress, render his forces lame, lost, hungry, thirsty... The three most generally employed tactics of guerilla warfare are : surprise attack, ambush and harassment. Fighting must be co-ordinated with sabotage. Sabotage is a wonderful means of resistance by guerilla forces or by regular troops less well-armed than the enemy.

Mobile warfare is fighting by the regular army, or by guerilla forces mustered into relatively big units and co-operating with the regular army, using more or less advanced weapons, concentrating themselves rapidly and launching lightning attacks : encircling the enemy in order to destroy him, working round positions to attack him, attacking rather from behind than launching frontal attacks, advancing rapidly and withdrawing quickly. On an extensive and deep battle front (sometimes stretching through the whole country), the fighting units must allocate duties among themselves and co-ordinate their actions, consistently attacking the enemy according to a common plan, disturbing his forces, spreading alarm and disorder among them, so that they do not know whether to run or to fight. The characteristic of mobile warfare is : *to manœuvre with flexibility to attack the enemy and destroy him.*

To win, we must wage guerilla war and mobile warfare or guerilla-and-mobile warfare ; that means, a mixed form of military tactic. But all this does not mean that we shall not practise positional warfare. *What is positional warfare ?* It is the method of deploying forces of the regular army in readiness for a battle, digging trenches, setting up fortifications, checking the enemy's advance, taking advantage of the enemy's weak points and inadequacies to attack him and occupy his positions.

So long as we are not so well-armed as the enemy, to apply positional warfare in a hurry is to doom ourselves to failure. That is why guerilla and mobile warfare are at present the chief forms of fighting, and positional warfare only a side-form. Concerning guerilla and mobile warfare, according to the objective, subjective and practical conditions at each particular time and place, guerilla warfare should sometimes be applied rather than mobile warfare, and sometimes *vice-versa*. Because we are short of arms, guerilla warfare will in general be the most widespread method of fighting employed by our people in the long-term resistance. With the gradual development of the war, our army will gain more experience and we shall have more modern arms, so that mobile warfare will be applied more extensively, until, finally, in the stage of general counter-offensive, positional warfare will play the paramount role.

As they have not yet thoroughly grasped the principles of the above-mentioned methods of fighting, our regular troops and guerilla forces often commit considerable tactical blunders. The Thi Nghe battle at the end of 1945, the Nha Trang and Thua Thien battles in early 1946, the battle to the west of Hanoi last March and others, have proved that in the first stages our troops had a tendency to fight a war of position. They therefore suffered losses or became bewildered when attacked by the enemy. On the [33] other hand, where we shift rapidly and in good time to guerilla and mobile warfare, we not only avoid losses but are also able to stay the advance of the enemy and to defeat him.

Guerilla warfare must be the tactic of the people as a whole, not of the army alone.

To achieve good results in guerilla and mobile warfare, we must mobilize the people to support our armed forces enthusiastically and to fight the enemy together with them. The people are the eyes and ears of the army, they feed and keep our soldiers. It is they who help the army in sabotage and in battle. *The people are the water and our*

---

[33] In the battles mentioned here (the first took place in the South, the other two in Central Viet-Nam), the Viet-Minh attempted to make a stand against French regulars and sustained heavy losses. This passage is a severe criticism of General Giap's tactics in these campaigns.

army the fish. The people constitute an inexhaustible source of strength to the army. To increase their numbers, the troops must recruit new fighters from among the people. That is why the entire people must be armed, guerilla movements must be initiated, the actions of the regular army and guerilla forces must be co-ordinated. We must act in such a way that wherever the enemy goes, he meets the resistance forces of the entire Vietnamese people who, arms in hand, fight against him, ready to die rather than return to slavery. [34]

[34] This paragraph clearly shows the influence of Mao Tse-tung's teachings. The sentence that precedes it is in itself an excellent definition of revolutionary warfare.

VI

RESISTANCE IN THE POLITICAL FIELD

To defeat the French invaders, knowing how to fight, or fighting skilfully, is not enough. It is necessary to have good home and foreign policies.

Within the country, the entire people must be united. The anti-French national united front must be consolidated and developed daily to oppose the aggressors.

To wage a long resistance war, the entire people must be united and single-minded. It is the same with our people as with a bundle of chopsticks. If the chopsticks are bound together it is difficult to break them. But if they are separated, nothing is easier than to snap them one by one until the last.

But uniting the whole people doesn't mean that we blithely shut our eyes and allow a handful of Vietnamese traitors to betray their country freely, that we permit them freely to sabotage the resistance, become the henchmen of the enemy, and deceive and massacre our compatriots. To fight the enemy and to crush the national traitors are two tasks which must be undertaken simultaneously.

At present, the French invaders are striving to deceive and divide our people. To sow discord between our Catholic and non-Catholic compatriots, they order their agents to make propaganda by telling the Catholic patriots that the Viet Minh are Communists, that the Ho Chi Minh Government is a Viet Minh Government and that to follow the Ho Chi Minh Government is to follow the Communists. They say that, later on if the impossible happened and the resistance was victorious, our Catholic compatriots would be forbidden to worship God, that the churches would be burnt and the crucifixes destroyed. "Rather lose one's country than one's God ; rather be enslaved than face eternal damnation."

Such misleading propaganda must be brought to nothing. Communism is a doctrine that hides neither its ends nor its means. But it is not our intention here to explain what Communism is. However, our Catholic compatriots should realize that the Ho Chi Minh Government is a government of the entire people, approved by the National Assembly. This resistance war is a revolutionary war of the entire people led by our government. It is not a private war concerning only the Communists or the Viet Minh Front. The Communists or the Viet Minh Front have the sole aim of gaining freedom and independence for Viet Nam. *This resistance will bring democratic freedoms to our people, including freedom of belief and freedom of religion.* It is those who bomb pagodas, desecrate the cross, and use churches as military posts from which to massacre our people, who spurn Christian charity. Those who rape Catholic nuns and kill Buddhist bonzes are not the Viet Minh or the Communists, but the French invaders. " *To love one's country is to serve God.* " If we love our country and serve God, how can we refrain from fighting the French invaders ?

The French bandits are doing their best to sow discord between the people of the South and those of the North, between the Thai, Nung, De, Muong, Man and Tho peoples and the majority people, between rich and poor. But facts have proved that they are doing so in order to occupy Nam Bo (south Viet Nam) ; *they are using Vietnamese to fight Vietnamese,* cutting Viet Nam up into pieces, inciting the minority peoples to oppose the majority people; they are egging on the Thai and Nung peoples to fight the majority people, and are using the latter to oppose the Thai and Nung peoples, to enable the colonialists to subjugate them all and in ease enjoy the position of " masters of the country ".

This resistance aims at wiping out the French colonialists, to win independence and national unification, to bring freedom and happiness to the entire people. The lives and property of the people will be respected. The living conditions of the labouring masses will be improved. Like all other democratic freedoms, freedom of belief is guaranteed. Our compatriots of the Centre, North and South are one ; all nationalities — minority as well as majority — are equal. The aim of the resistance is clear. The French invaders cannot hoodwink our people !

The French bandits even declare that they are *"fighting the Viet Minh and not Viet Nam."* But in fact they are prejudicing the lives and property of the Vietnamese people — Viet Minh or non - Viet Minh — without discrimination ! They seek to divide the Viet Minh from the entire people, because they know that the Viet Minh consists of the most patriotic and determined elements in the country. They are the most faithful to the people's interests. They sacrifice themselves to struggle to the end for national independence and unification. The enemy knows clearly that he can subdue our people only if the Viet Minh is isolated, if they succeed in inciting the people to oppose the Viet Minh.

On the one hand, the French invaders deceive and divide our people. On the other, they massacre and rob them. That is why, from their own experience, our people clearly recognize the hypocritical face of the enemy and are closing their ranks day by day, supporting the Viet Minh, joining it and the Lien Viet Front, and, together with the Viet Minh, fighting against the enemy. We thank the French for contributing, by their words and deeds, to speeding up the movement of " transforming the Vietnamese people into Viet Minh ".

The basis of our national resistance front is already in existence. By violating the right to live of the Vietnamese people, the reactionary French colonialists have unwittingly consolidated and further developed this basis. It is necessary to help the people to see for what they are, the perfidious schemes of the French aggressors, at the same time skilfully making use of every possibility, big or small, of contributing to the resistance ; thus our policy of wide national unity will certainly succeed.

At home, national unity must be maintained; the national united front against the French colonialists and their lackeys must be consolidated and developed. This front must be built on the cornerstone of the alliance of the workers and peasants, and must be led by the working class. Concerning our foreign policy, what must our people do ? We must isolate the enemy, win more friends. We must act in such a way that the French people and the French colonial peoples will actively support us and oppose the reactionary French colonialists, that all peace-loving forces in the world will defend us and favour the aims of our resistance. That is why French prisoners-of-war and all foreign residents in our country must be well-treated (leaving aside the bandits who use their situation as foreign residents to work as lackeys of the French colonialists).

The French people and soldiers have been deceived by the reactionary French colonialists and led to believe that we violated the Agreements and attacked France first. We must bring to their notice irrefutable proof to make them understand that the reactionary French colonialists trampled on the Agreements and attacked us first. They not only want to exploit our people again but they are also exploiting the French people. To fight the French colonialists is to help the French people directly, because while fighting we weaken our common enemy. The French people and soldiers should oppose the war by every means : oppose the sending of troops to Indochina, oppose military expenditure for the reconquest of Viet Nam, for these are actions which are completely contrary to the new Constitution of France ; they should demand from the French Government peaceful negotiations with the Ho Chi Minh Government. The French soldiers in Viet Nam should demand repatriation, protest against the setting up of a puppet Government, fraternize with the Vietnamese People's Army, and turn their arms against the reactionary French colonialists, joining the ranks of the Vietnamese army and people in order to fight hand in hand with them for the overthrow of the common enemy of our two peoples. This will enable an independent and unified Viet Nam to form a voluntary alliance with the new France on the basis of equality and mutual benefit.

We must make the people in the French colonies realize that while we are fighting the reactionary French colonialists, we are, to a certain extent, fighting for them too. Therefore, they should seize the opportunity presented by the predicament of the French colonialists in Viet Nam to rise up and recover their own independence.

We must make the progressive forces all over the world realize that we are making sacrifices and exerting efforts for the cause of world peace and democracy too. In the struggle for peace and democracy, these forces cannot remain indifferent to our struggle or support Viet Nam only by words where deeds are required. They must arraign France before the tribunal of world opinion to judge her and compel her stop the war of rapine in Indochina, a war completely contrary to the ideals of the United Nations Charter. Moreover, they should help the Indochinese peoples from the material as well as the moral point of view, so as rapidly to crush the reactionary French colonialists, sworn enemies of world peace and democracy.

The tasks of the resistance from the political point of view are extremely heavy. To fulfil them, on the one hand we must consolidate the democratic republican State, strengthen the machinery of resistance, and *unify all military, administrative, and popular organizations in the whole country ;* all patriotic organizations must be developed, the leading machinery of the people's resistance consolidated ; military questions must be subordinated to political leadership. On the other hand, *all traitors, wreckers, opportunists, cowards, bureaucrats, militarist and factionalist elements must be thrown out of the machinery of resistance, traitors must be punished, the seeds of disruption and division among the people destroyed, and the political rear consolidated to the highest degree.* The following goals must be our constant concern :

To unite the entire people ;

To isolate the enemy ;

To guarantee victory in the resistance.

VII

RESISTANCE IN THE ECONOMIC FIELD

To fight the enemy, we must eat our fill, be healthy and have great qualities of endurance. That is why particular importance must be attached to economic problems and the people's living conditions.

To enable the people to fight the enemy resolutely, we must improve their living standards while fighting. If the people are poverty-stricken and lack adequate political consciousness, they may be deceived by the enemy.

The enemy does not fight us in the military and political fields alone, but also in the economic field. For instance, they blockade and pillage us, and sabotage our arrangements for food supplies. We too must fight them in the economic field. An economic plan for the long term resistance must be drawn up. The economy of the resistance war must be built so that we will gradually gain on the enemy's economy.

Mao Tse-tung, the revolutionary leader of China, has said : " *To put aside economy and only to speak of revolution is to commit suicide, but not to touch a hair of the enemy.* " (Mao Tse-tung : *On Economic and Financial Problems.*)

Our resistance in the economic field consists of two parts : passive and active. The passive side consists in sabotaging the enemy's economy, and the active side in building our own.

How should we sabotage the enemy's economy in our country ? There are many ways : blowing up his machines, warehouses and lines of communication and transport, so that he cannot enjoy in peace the wealth extorted from the people by exploitation ; opposing his policy of rapine, not allowing him to " use war to feed war ". (This manœuvre, incidentally, is not peculiar to the Japanese fascists, it is the common practice of all aggressors.)

We should act in such a way that wherever the enemy goes, he meets scenes of scorched earth, with nothing left for him to pillage. The more the enemy extends the front, the greater the danger to his food supplies, and the more the war becomes a burden to him.

If we never budge an inch from the people, if we arm the whole nation, if we become masters of the countryside, not only can we check the enemy's attempts to destroy our economy, but we can also sabotage his. At the same time, we will build our own economy.

The building of our economy must be directed in accordance with the two following principles :

1. Simultaneously with the resistance war, national reconstruction must be carried out.

2. Self-supply must be worked for in every field.

Concerning the first principle, we should keep in mind that we must not wait until after the victory of the resistance to start the reconstruction of our country. We must carry out reconstruction in the course of the resistance war itself ; we will reconstruct in order to be able to carry on the resistance.

Our economy in the period of the resistance is a war economy in form, and a new democratic economy in content. This means that on the one hand the people's economic life must meet the conditions of war ; every economic activity must aim at guaranteeing the supply of the front, and providing the whole people with all the commodities necessary to carry on the long resistance (war form of our economy). On the other hand, individual economy, co-operative economy and State economy * must be simultaneously developed. We should skilfully use the co-operative economy as a link between the individual economy and the State economy. We should improve the living standards of the people to enable them to take part enthusiastically in developing the economy and supplying the army and our compatriots (new democratic content of our economy).

---

* Individual economy means ownership by individuals or families ; co-operative economy means ownership by many people who invest capital together and work together ; State economy means ownership by the State.

Apart from these forms, we may organize yet another form, that of "joint State-private enterprises ", in which the State and the private capitalists invest capital together.

In our resistance economy, to what should we attach particular importance ?

The development of agriculture must receive our closest attention, because our country lives by agriculture. Nearly all the needs of the people are supplied by agriculture. Then come handicrafts. We must encourage handicrafts and small industry to produce articles capable of replacing industrial products. Commerce ranks third. We should develop small trade, organize and carefully control foreign trade. At the same time, we must act in such a way that the co-operatives shoulder an important part of the tasks connected with distribution and consumption. For us, industry can rank only fourth, although it plays a rather important role in war in modern times. We should pay particular attention to industries producing weapons, and those which process raw materials which we have available.

Keen attention must be paid to the development of cattle-breeding alongside agriculture, and of transport alongside handicrafts. The war extends every day, roads and bridges are destroyed daily : if we do not establish a system of transport adapted to the new situation, production and distribution of products will suffer disastrously.

As far as the second principle, that of self-supply, is concerned, we realize clearly that our country is an agricultural country, and that even if we lose all the cities and suffer enemy blockade, we will still be able to ensure our self-supply. (This does not mean that the enemy will be permitted freely to occupy all the cities, or completely blockade us.) Our country is endowed with plenty of raw materials and manpower, the spirit of our people is high, thus we can build a self-sufficient economy along the following lines.

Raising production norms — We must improve technique and methods of production, reducing the number of idlers. Excepting particular cases, armymen, students and office employees should also take part in production to a certain extent.

Producing according to war-time needs — During the resistance war, we produce what we need, not luxury goods. For example, we produce rice, salt, cloth, guns, bullets, etc., but not scent and toilet soap.

Building the State economy and the co-operative economy according to a plan. In our present conditions, we cannot have a completely planned economy, but at least all branches of production and distribution must be readjusted and put under unified guidance, although individual initiative is free to develop. And the enterprises managed by the State, and all co-operatives, *can produce according to a plan.*

To achieve good results in the resistance in the economic field, we must define an economic policy for this period. In our opinion, that policy should meet the following needs :

1 — *To increase production* — We should initiate a movement of patriotic competition for increasing production, arouse the people's eagerness in labour, and mobilize all our manpower, material and financial resources. Except in some special areas, militia men must cleave close to the fields to plough them. (When the enemy comes we fight, when he goes we plough.) The aim of raising production during the resistance war consists in the three points of *eating one's fill, dressing adequately, and having strength to fight.* Work exchange and co-operation in production must

be encouraged and developed. We should transfer the refugees, particularly those who have production skills, from the regions ravaged by war to areas that are relatively safe, have land available but lack manpower, in order to set up farms for shock-production. We must pay particular attention to the supply of rice, salt, medicines, oxen, buffaloes and farming implements to such farms.

2 — *To increase income, cut costs, and practise thrift.* A war budget must be prepared. The two main sources of income for this budget are the various taxes, and the income from the State enterprises. Taxes must be collected according to the democratic principle : the rich pay more, the poor pay less, the very poor are exempt from tax. To balance the budget we must increase income and bring down expenditure. A policy of thrift must be put into effect. In the administrative and military departments, in all organisations and among the people, non-essential expenditures must be done away with. The number of civil servants will be reduced. If we must spend, we will spend boldly ; but our spending must be reasonable, our draft budget must be highly precise.

3 — *To gradually lighten the people's burden.* Taxes and rates, etc., must be reduced to lighten the burden borne by the people. At the same time, we must carry out step by step our land policy with a view to improving the peasants' life, because the peasants are the greatest reservoir of manpower and of material strength for the resistance.

4 — *Exhortation, reward and punishment.* Even when our plans are good, if we do not know how to mobilize and encourage the people to carry them out, the people will certainly not take part in carrying them out as a body. In every field there are people who work well and people who

work badly. To forgo rewards and punishments would be an error. That is why we should organize exibitions of products and crafts, institute medals to be awarded to Labour Heroes, talented inventors and those who are rich in goodwill. At the same time, we should severely punish the thieves of public property, the speculators, smugglers, and saboteurs, confiscate the property of the national traitors and use such property to improve the people's life.

5 — *Consolidating the currency, stabilizing prices.* We must maintain the value of our currency, avoid inflation, and use Vietnamese currency in production. (We will exchange home products and goods for necessary foreign goods which we cannot yet produce ourselves.) The Government must ensure the supply of staple commodities such as rice, salt, cloth, etc., to all government departments, to the troops and to the people, with a view to keeping prices steady.

To put into effect the above-mentioned policies, we must fight against wrong ideas concerning economy, and against the tendency to demagogy consisting in the abolition of all taxes. This error was committed in many places after the August uprising. We must also struggle against the tendency towards extortion of money from the people, obliging them to make too heavy contributions ; against the style of work of planlessness, of working in a happy-go-lucky manner, of scratching where it itches, paying attention to the pipe only where it is leaking, or making grandiose plans and extensive programmes without being able to achieve them. We should fight the tendency to passivity, as it exists among those who do not think about developing the economy and further exploiting our rich resources, but only about practising extreme stinginess. We must oppose waste, disorder, corruption and degeneracy, fighting against the " left " deviation in economic affairs of those who can think only of " agricultural collectivization ", and the building of a heavy war industry, and under-estimate agriculture and handicrafts, and who thus get confused and waste considerable time and effort in elaborating illusory plans which can in no way be carried out in our conditions.

VIII

RESISTANCE IN THE CULTURAL FIELD

Resistance in the military, political, and economic fields is not enough for our all-out resistance. We must also wage resistance in the cultural field. Culture is also a battle-front of our people. The tasks of the resistance in the cultural field consist in :

1. — Doing away with obscurantist culture, introduced by the French colonialists to strengthen their domination.

2. — Building a new democratic culture for Viet Nam.

How is the obscurantist culture of the French colonialists to be done away with ? (Let us never confuse this kind of culture with the genuine and progressive culture of the French people.)

Of course, the resistance of our people is wiping out the evil influence of this reactionary culture. The slavish, cowardly and parasitic ways of the French time are being wiped out. The moral and intellectual fetters used by the French colonialists are being smashed. But we must realize that the colonialist culture remains prevalent in the habits and thoughts of our cadres and people. The French colonialists will still deceive our people as long as they exist in our country. Every day, the pamphlets, books, newspapers, magazines, speeches and radio of the enemy sow their poison among our people, so that there are still some to be found among us who believe that the enemy has good intentions. There are people who have doubts as to our final victory, or even believe that the enemy's " mission " is to fight us in order to re-establish peace and order, to bring the light of civilization to our people, and so on. These myths, decked out in cultural forms, are backed by the policy of armed terror and economic corruption, and have been of some advantage to the enemy, particularly in the occupied zones.

This is very dangerous ! We must resolutely fight it.

Now, all artists and writers, all teachers and all intellectuals must take part in the resistance, open up a cultural front, attack the cultural strongholds of the enemy.

At present, in the rear, our engineers, together with the workers are striving all-out to produce arms, to establish workshops and production camps to produce what is necessary for the army and the people. Doctors, medical men and students are taking care of the wounded soldiers and of the health of the cadres and the masses. A number of architects are taking part in the construction of defence works, office building and reception centres for evacuees. Thus, they are participating in the resistance.

All our teachers are striving to free the people from illiteracy and to train cadres in service of the long resistance. Our musicians are composing martial and inspiring works. Our poets are writing poems which arouse hatred of the enemy. A number of artists and painters are zealously participating in propaganda work for the resistance. Thus, they are taking part in the resistance, too, aren't they?

All political figures, journalists and writers are stimulating the army and people to unite for the struggle, clearly pointing out the advantages and disadvantages of political lines, proposing tactics, lines and policies. Is resistance of this kind any less important than going to the front with arms?

But all this is not enough. Further efforts must be made. There still exist many shortcomings in our cultural activity. All the cultural forces at our disposal, all the talented writers, scientists and artists, are not yet fully mobilized. Numbers of cultural workers want to work, but do not know what to do; there are even people who are still indifferent. Those cultural workers who have boldly taken part in the resistance, and are serving the army and mingling with the people, have recorded more or less great progress. But we feel that they have not yet a clear-cut guiding principle and plan.

The enemy is trampling on our fatherland. The whole nation is struggling heroically. At present, every cultural activity must be in line with this slogan : " Love for the country and hatred for the enemy. "

All cultural workers must celebrate and work for the renewal of the collective heroism of the people, arousing to the greatest extent hatred among our army and people for the enemy, in order to equip them to go eagerly forward to fight the enemy, preferring death to surrender. Their work must aim at welding our people into one bloc in support of the Government, having firm confidence in national salvation, not losing heart when faced with difficulties and hardships. Their work must aim at doing everything to dishearten the enemy troops, depressing their morale, causing them to leave the enemy and to pass over to our ranks, to the right path.

The measures to be taken to achieve the above aims are numerous. Our cultural workers must make frequent use of the simplest forms, capable of winning a ready response from the masses ; for instance : sketches, pictures, dances, newspapers (particularly wall-newspapers), leaflets, talks, etc.

We are not afraid to use the forms of propaganda of the old culture which are familiar to the broad masses, the forms most effective in influencing them ; for example, the various folk song styles such as " Trong quan ", " Quan ho ", " Hat dum " and " Hat boi ", should be widely used, provided that we give them a new content and a new artistic spirit.

Using culture in service of the resistance in such a way is to build a new culture for the country.

In our opinion, that culture must be based on the three following principles :

a — It must be national ;
b — It must be scientific ;
c — It must be popular.

What is contrary to national, scientific and popular principles, either in form or in content, must be eliminated.

The war partly helps us in this work. Indeed, this war is a great upheaval. It helps us to boldly "revolutionize" culture. Big events are taking place : many towns are being destroyed, townspeople are evacuating to the countryside. The towns, which were formerly the cultural centres, are now occupied by the enemy and are being turned into dark and savage places, abounding in the depraved, obscurantist "culture" of the aggressors. In contrast, the countryside, formerly a dark and backward place, is now becoming civilized and progressive. Culture was formerly a thing enjoyed by a handful of rich people in the cities ; it has now, in a short time, come closer to the broad masses. In order to serve the Fatherland and the people, cultural workers must create works which are simple, and well-adapted to the level of the people, who, for the most part, are illiterate, or have only very little education. (Their works must be *popular*.) In this time of war, old elaborate forms and habits, ill-adapted to the new times — bureaucracy is an outstanding instance — tend to disappear ; in the resistance, every task must be rationally and economically performed, and it must serve a purpose. What is not scientific tends to disappear. (Our cultural works must be *scientific*.)

The resistance stirs up our hatred against everything anti-national, against everything which apes the colonialists. In this situation, cultural workers are able rapidly to gain an understanding of their slavish diseases of the "half breed French" and the "half-breed Chinese" in order to cure themselves. (Our cultural works must be *national*.)

Good opportunities exist. The conditions of the resistance are very favourable to the building of a new culture. It requires only that the Vietnamese cultural workers boldly rise up, and avail themselves of the opportunity to develop Vietnamese culture on the basis of new democracy. Here are their practical tasks :

a — To use art and literature for propaganda and for mobilization of the forces of the resistance ;

b — To struggle against illiteracy ;

c — To build a new life ;

d — To popularize the practice of hygiene among the people ;

e — To wipe out all slavish, colonialist remnants in the cultural field ;

f — To develop a culture having a national, scientific and popular character.

To advance, our cultural circles must engage in a severe self-criticism, and give up their tendencies to self-esteem to despise the masses and to be divorced from them. They should shake off the tendencies to wavering and opportunism. Regarding traditional culture and foreign culture, we should refrain from mere invective in dealing with these matters ; but we should not follow their examples blindly. We should have a critical spirit, assimilating what is good in other cultures, and rejecting what is bad.

In this great struggle, those who fail to keep pace with the movement, who do not adapt themselves to the rapidly changing situation, will certainly be left far behind. Our cultural workers should pay close attention to this fact.

IX

CHARACTERISTICS OF THE WAR

We have so far described four sides (military, political, economic and cultural) of the war against the French. Now, on the basis of the military situation in our country during these last months, we take up the question of the characteristics of this war.

War of interlocking — Our resistance war is a people's[35] war : regular army, militia and guerilla forces combine and fight together. Regular forces launch frontal attacks and guerillas fight from the rear, thus catching the enemy between two fires. Sometimes the regular army is obliged to withdraw to maintain its forces, but then militia forces and a small part of the regular army turn themselves into guerilla groups, hiding behind the enemy's lines to fight ;

---

[35] The awkward term "interlocking" used here is translated in the French edition as *"guerre en dents de peigne,"* i.e., a war whose various phases and fronts are as intertwined as two combs stuck into each other. The terms "entangled" or "dovetailed" could also be used, but Truong Chinh, as is shown on the following pages, seeks to convey the idea of the constant infiltration and counterinfiltration of which this type of war consists.

or considerable regular forces attack quickly under cover of night, penetrating very deeply into enemy-held areas, launching lightning attacks on bases considered by the enemy to be quite secure. After fulfilling their task, they withdraw according to a plan, cheating the enemy's attempts to encircle and annihilate them. The attacks launched by our troops on Ha Dong (March 20, 1947 and April 13, 1947) on Haiphong (March 22, 1947) * and recently on the Viet Nam University students hostels in Hanoi (April 20, 1947), taking place long after our withdrawal from these cities, are striking examples of this.

As for the enemy, they use motorized infantry to break through at many points deep into our zones, or work round our positions over a rather big area, hoping to encircle and annihilate our troops, destroy our bases, plunder our property and sow bewilderment among us. Sometimes they send paratroops and commandos to cities or bases far from the battlefield, in our rear-lines to occupy these places, hoping to hinder our communications and supply lines, or to open another front in our rear. The paratroop raid made by the enemy at Hoa Binh on April 15, 1947 provides food for thought in this connection.

Thus the enemy attacks deep behind our lines, and we launch attacks deep behind his. This war has the characteristic of two combs whose teeth are interlocked.

Disorderly war — In many regions in the delta, the [36] enemy fights us not only in the military field but also strives to destroy us in the economic field; they pillage crops and destroy harvests, hoping to drive our people to surrender out of utter poverty. In certain very narrow

---

* Occupied at this time by the French forces (Ed.)

[36] Here, the French term is *"mêlées confuses."* The word "melee" used in its English sense would have conveyed the same meaning.

regions, pressed between mountains and sea (such as the Binh Tri Thien zone and the southernmost part of Central[37] Viet Nam), the enemy attacks us at both ends, then cuts the regions into parts in which he launches mopping-up operations.

In these regions, experience has taught us that to avoid disintegration, our troops should quickly abandon their uniforms, combine with the people, distribute a part of their arms to them, organize militia forces, arm the entire people, using every means to fight the enemy. They should cling to the rice-fields and struggle against the enemy to win the right to live. The army and the people must unite into one bloc to wage a mortal combat against the Expeditionary Corps at any time and anywhere.

Thus the war has the characteristics of " disorder ", muddle and fierceness.

War without battle-fronts — The result of the inter locking and disorderly war above-described is a war without battle-fronts between the enemy troops and ourselves or a war in which the battle-front is not clearly defined. The character of the fighting is constantly changing. Our army and militia forces fight the enemy everywhere, sometimes in his rear, sometimes right in his midst. Sometimes, the enemy advances into our zone, our forces strike at him from behind and at his flanks rather than launching frontal attacks, wearing him out by forcing him to ward off blows.

The battle-front is rather extensive ; but even quite close to Hanoi, Haiphong, Saigon, Cholon, our troops constantly attack enemy posts. As day after day, we arm the entire people and initiate the guerilla movements, the enemy has to fight for every step forward ; our troops and gueril-las open a battle-front wherever they encounter the enemy.

---

[37] Binh-Tri-Thien was a Viet-Minh stronghold extending over parts of the provinces of Quang-Binh, Quang-Tri, and Thua-Thien, straddling the 17th parallel.

Not only in areas under our control, but even in his own occupied zones he cannot consolidate his rear.

Every guerilla base or nucleus in enemy-held regions at a given time will also have its front and rear lines. The positions of these bases, and their front and rear lines, are constantly changing.

A war without rear lines, without clear front lines — this is another particular characteristic of the war against the French colonialists.

War of encirclement — Due to his possession of naval forces the enemy controls the territorial waters and coastal regions. He occupies a number of cities close to the frontier. Thus we are encircled by the enemy. But when all-out war broke out, when he wished to attack us with his forces already stationed on our soil, the cities in which enemy forces were garrisoned and all enemy positions were immediately encircled by our forces. During the first two months, the Hanoi battle showed an unusual reciprocal encirclement carried out by the enemy forces and by our own : the enemy encircled us in the centre of the city, and we encircled the enemy in the suburbs.

The enemy seeks to occupy many cities and major communication lines, setting up a system of encirclement to surround us. But when he breaks through our encirclement around the towns and penetrates into the countryside, or parachutes forces into our free zone, his forces are immediately encircled by ours.

Our guerilla bases in the enemy-held regions can appear to be mere enclaves surrounded by the enemy. But all these guerilla bases, together with the broad free zones, form a huge net encircling the enemy in return.

Let us look at the world pattern. The enemy seeks to appeal to the imperialist forces to encircle us (D'Argenlieu appeals to the British and Americans for help in fighting the "Vietnamese Communists"). Together with the democratic, progressive, peaceful forces the world over, with the oppressed peoples in Asia (first of all the Khmer and Laotian peoples) with the French people and all the peoples of the French colonies who are struggling for national liberation, we are encircling the aggressive French colonialists. The enemy is encircled on our soil, in France, in the French Union and in the world. We see that he is many times surrounded. In this mutual encirclement, those who enjoy the support and sympathy of the Indochinese peoples and the peoples the world over will carry the day.

War of scorched earth -- What is beneficial to the enemy and harmful to us must be burnt down or destroyed, if it cannot be kept for ourselves. That is the principle of "resistance by scorched earth". The scorched earth tactic is not a Vietnamese invention but the scale on which we have applied it has been a big surprise to many people. There are foreigners who think that it is madness for the Vietnamese people, of their own will, to raze towns and cities, with their own hands to set ablaze not only the quarters and storehouses of the enemy, but their own houses as well. Now, the Vietnamese people are not mad. If the Vietnamese people have applied scorched earth tactics to a degree unusual in the history of people's wars, they have their reasons for doing so :

a) Generally speaking, the Vietnamese people are weaker than the enemy in arms and equipment, that is why they should destroy bridges and roads to check or slow down the advance of the enemy's motorized infantry.

b) With their high spirit, the Vietnamese people can make great sacrifices, provided that they cause difficulties to the enemy and bring his defeat closer. The Vietnamese people realize clearly that the task of sabotage is as important as fighting at the front. Sabotage is a means of fighting of a people armed with rudimentary weapons, against aggressors who are more inured to war and possess higher technique.

Apart from the above-mentioned factors the scorched earth tactic brings us other advantages. For instance : it causes the enemy to despair, because each time he thinks he is going to occupy a town or a city, he can finally take over only heaps of rubble and ashes. It displays to the enemy the determination of our people to wage the resistance war, and to defend their freedom.

The more the French invaders and the Vietnamese traitors curse the tactic of scorched earth, the more clearly they show us that this tactic hurts them very much because it strikes right at their greed by preventing them from filling their pockets. In their propaganda, they wail that our High Command orders application of scorched earth tactics " to achieve communism, wiping out the difference between rich and poor ". What a crude lie ! Our people know very well that when the last reactionary colonialist is driven out of Viet Nam, with our rich resources, the creative spirit of the toiling people and with the skilful organization and leadership of the democratic Government, fine buildings and cities of new design will gradually appear on the soil of independent Viet Nam. And, at present, in many places, the French invaders pillage our compatriots without discrimination between rich and poor. Is it not they in fact who " wipe out the difference between rich and poor " ?

In our country, scorched earth tactics are dictated by the circumstances of our resistance, by the relation of forces between the enemy and ourselves, by the quantity of our arms and by our spirit. Scorched earth resistance thoroughly carried out on a large scale is another particular characteristic of the present war against the French.

In short, the anti-French war is an utterly destructive and frightful war. The enemy is ferocious and we are fearless. The two sides are engaged in a deadly hand-to-hand fight, determined to decide victory and defeat. Thus, the war against the French has a number of quite distinctive characteristics.

X

THE THREE STAGES OF THE
LONG-TERM RESISTANCE

In Chapter V, we dealt with the reasons why we must wage a long resistance, why we must prolong our fight to win victory. Our long resistance will pass through three stages :

1) The stage of contention,[38]

2) The stage of equilibrium,

3) The stage of general counter-offensive.

Here we cannot describe in detail all the steps forward of the resistance. We can only map out general lines.

a) *The stage of contention* — Because, at the beginning, the enemy forces are stronger than ours, the enemy's strategy is offensive and ours is defensive. The enemy occupies a number of towns and main communication lines,

---

[38] The French text uses the word *"défensive,"* which is considerably different in meaning from "contention."

the coastal region and some areas of the delta. After waging a fierce resistance and encircling the enemy in these regions our troops are obliged to withdraw to *safeguard their forces ;* in particularly favourable circumstances, they will lure the enemy to penetrate deep into our rear to attack him.

But we do not always withdraw, letting the enemy freely extend his security zone around the cities under his temporary control, and consolidate the communications and supply lines between occupied towns.

Our strategy is defensive, but our tactics and campaigning principles are constantly to attack. In the whole country, we withdraw to prepared positions, but locally we continue to attack, launching sudden assaults on enemy positions right in the heart of his occupied zones (for example, the attack on Gia Lam airport on January 16, 1947, the battles in Ha Dong and Haiphong in March and April 1947, etc).

During this period, the military aim of the enemy is to control the big cities and main communication lines, control the coastal region, the frontier and the delta, cut up our country into many parts, hinder our supply and communications, hoping to annihilate our regular forces, and destroy our bases, enterprises and storehouses. In the political field, they make deceitful propaganda, accusing us of violating agreements and attacking them first in order to justify their aggressive acts before the people of France and the world. Simultaneously, they seek to sow discord between the Viet Minh and the people, to entice evacuated compatriots back to the occupied zones, and to set up puppet administrations in the occupied cities and around them.

To achieve these political and military aims, they mobilize their air and land forces, including motorized infantry, applying the tactics of positional and mobile warfare, launching lightning attacks, working round our positions, attacking us in pincer movements, launching parachute raids or landing troops to attack us (the battles in Haiphong, and Hai Duong of December 1946, in Thua Thien and Quang Tri of February 1947, Ha Dong of March 1947, etc.) At the same time, they buy up Vietnamese national traitors and bandits, deceive our Catholic compatriots and followers of the Hoa Hao and Cao Dai sects, and bribe national minority people.

Our forces are still small in number, weak in equipment, and not yet inured to war ; but they have a high spirit and enjoy the support of the people. Moreover, they know from the beginning how to apply flexible tactics, that is why on the one hand they can maintain their strength and on the other hand wear out the enemy forces and damage their prestige, thus bringing the enemy's schemes to partial failure. Simultaneously, we mobilize the people to rise up for resistance. We strive to consolidate the unity within our ranks, unite the entire people, unmask the enemy, win the sympathy and support of the French people and the people the world over, show them clearly our will for peace and the circumstances which oblige our people to fight in self-defence.

Here are our tactics during this stage : at first, we apply positional warfare in the streets, holding on to every house, every street or every quarter (battles in Hanoi, Nam Dinh, Hue). Then we withdraw from the towns, using positional warfare tactics to bottle the enemy up in the towns for a certain time (battle in Hanoi etc.) Simultaneously, small units of our forces penetrate into the streets, using guerilla warfare to harass the enemy. Guerilla warfare fosters and helps positional warfare.

Gradually, the enemy extends his attacks from the big towns, and occupies more towns and communication lines. As this process goes on, the war of position passes to second place, giving way to guerilla and mobile warfare. Positional warfare fosters and helps guerilla and mobile warfare. It is still necessary to stop the enemy's advance. But if we have resort only to positional warfare, the enemy will use mobile warfare to work round our positions or encircle us, thus causing us big losses. Generally speaking, during the stage of contention, compared with guerilla warfare, mobile warfare plays the leading part. But gradually, towards the end of this stage, the enemy-occupied zones being extended, and the militia and the guerilla movement having developed, guerilla warfare comes to play the major role.

b) The stage of equilibrium — Gradually the enemy's forces and our own become equal, the enemy strategy at this stage is to remain on the defensive, while ours is to prepare for the general counter-offensive. Generally speaking, the enemy no longer has sufficient strength to advance. To a certain extent he must call a halt, or make a few steps forward and then withdraw to his former positions. In general, we no longer have to retreat, but we have not yet sufficient strength to seize back the lost areas (although we can take back some positions). The two sides seem to be holding each other in the same positions. But the enemy's forces and ours do not only simply watch one other, like the stork and the oyster *. We continue to carry out partial attacks on the enemy-occupied zones. The result of many small attacks is equal to that of a big attack. As for the enemy, he does not remain constantly on the defensive and leave us in peace either. On the contrary, he is always carrying out raids in the occupied zones and launching spearhead attacks, deep into our free zones.

The military aim of the enemy during this stage is to consolidate his positions and communication lines, use relatively big forces to launch terrorist " mopping up " operations, hoping to " re-establish order " in the occupied zones. He strives to encircle and raze our guerilla bases there to blockade us, or chop up our free zones into many parts to destroy them, send agents into our zone to spy on the garrisoning of our troops, our settlements, storehouses, workshops, schools, etc, then to rain bombs on them or direct their henchmen to sabotage them. Their political aim is to set up a puppet national government, and Ky ** governments, at the same time fostering the puppet power in the localities and the organizations of reactionary notables, in order to divide and deceive our people, to induce our people to submit to them. They count on this puppet power, and its " armed forces " to repress our movement for liberation, and to pillage our people. Sitting on the necks of the puppet clique, they hope to enjoy in peace the fruits of their exploitation.

---

* The author refers to a Vietnamese fable : a stork wished to eat an oyster, but found that the oyster caught its bill and held it firmly. Thus, they remained, watching one another for a long time. A fisherman coming on the scene caught them both.

** Name given by the French to the three parts of Viet Nam : North, Centre, and South.

Our military and political aim during this stage is to wear out the enemy forces, annihilate them piecemeal ; sabotage, disturb, give the enemy no peace to exploit the people easily ; mobilize the people to wage armed struggle against the puppet administration, oppose the enemy's mopping-up policy and strive to annihilate bandits and traitors. Armed propaganda must be carried out on a large scale, particularly in the enemy-held region, to maintain the people's morale. We exert ourselves to overcome the weariness, discouragement, and tendencies to compromise and defeatism which may appear in the ranks of the resistance. Our aim is also to strengthen our forces, training more cadres, producing more weapons, establishing more regular and guerilla forces, developing and consolidating revolutionary organizations preparing conditions for the switch-over to the stage of general counter-offensive.

Our tactic during this stage is to apply guerilla warfare to the greatest possible extent, with a view to making it difficult for the enemy to eat and sleep, obliging his forces to scatter, tiring them and wearing them out. On the one hand a part of the regular forces must be set aside to organize, together with the people, guerilla forces, and to carry out guerilla warfare. On the other, regular troops must be concentrated at "mobile" spots, where the enemy must pass by, at places where "we can attack while advancing, or keep the position while retreating", at so-called " hinge " points, to attack isolated enemy posts, encircling and annihilating a part of the enemy's forces at the right time. Moreover, we launch sudden attacks on towns where enemy forces are not numerous.

The regular troops, militia and guerilla forces always co-ordinate their attacks, catching the enemy in a vice.

Thus, generally speaking, during the stage of equilibrium and in the whole country, guerilla warfare is the most widespread tactic, mobile warfare comes after it, following a period in which they are both of equal importance. Positional warfare plays the auxiliary role and helps guerilla and mobile warfare. By the end of this stage, a part of our guerilla warfare is being turned into mobile warfare, which is thereby reinforced.

This second stage is an extremely hard and complicated one, it is a relatively long stage but it is also the key stage, because it is then that we pass from an inferior position to a superior one to go forward to the stage of general counter-offensive.

c) *The stage of general counter-offensive* — In this stage, the balance of forces having changed in our favour, our strategy is to launch a general counter-offensive, and the enemy's strategy is to defend and retreat.

There are two factors determining our strategy of general counter-offensive. First, the strength of our army and people, and second, the weakening of the enemy and the extreme demoralisation of his troops. It may happen that our material forces are still not superior to those of the enemy. Granted that our material forces are even relatively weaker than the enemy's, still, as a result of the special conditions in Indochina, France, in the French colonies and the world over, and the tendency to disintegration in the enemy's morale, we can switch over to the stage of general counter-offensive.

For example, as a result of the long war the enemy troops become weary and discouraged, and are tormented by home-sickness. The French economy and finances are exhausted ; supplying the army is difficult, the French troops have to put up with privations, the French people do not want the war in Viet Nam to go on any longer. The movement against the war and against the diehards in France grows stronger and more fierce. The peoples in the colonies rise up actively against the French rulers. World opinion severely condemns France, which is isolated diplomatically. The world movement for peace and democracy scores great successes, etc. Such factors would have considerable influence on our liberation struggle, and create many favourable conditions for us in launching the general counter-offensive.[39]

As for us, although our material resources are not yet adequate, our fighting spirit soars constantly higher. Our army and people become more united. The solidarity of the entire people is strengthened daily.

With such subjective and objective conditions, the success of our ·general counter-offensive can be guaranteed.

During this stage, the enemy surrenders many positions and withdraws to entrench himself in the big cities. He will possibly hold false negotiations with us with a view to gaining time, carrying out delaying schemes in order to wait for direct and more active. assistance from world reaction. As for us, our consistent aim is that the whole country should rise up and go over to the offensive on all fronts, completely defeat the enemy and achieve true independence and unification.

As far as tactics are concerned, during this stage mobile warfare at first plays the outstanding role and is fostered and helped by guerilla warfare. Guerilla warfare is rapidly and extensively transformed into mobile warfare (many guerilla groups gathered together form units analogous to those of the regular forces and apply mobile warfare).

[39] General Giap (and probably Ho and Pham Van Dong as well) misread the timetable this paragraph contains. In the spring of 1951, Giap launched three major attacks with his raw divisions against Marshal de Lattre de Tassigny's forces. All three attacks failed completely. But by 1954, the "objective conditions" of which Truong Chinh speaks did materialize, and the French were defeated.

Mobile warfare is in its turn transformed into positional warfare. Battles for cities and strongpoints take place all the time, finally after a number of campaigns, mobile changes into positional warfare, which plays the predominant role in the last, decisive phase.

Our troops concentrate rapidly and actively launch planned lightning attacks on the cities and the enemy positions to encircle and annihilate them. In brief, we throw all our forces throughout the country into the battle to crush the enemy completely and win back the whole of our territory ! The machinery of enemy rule temporarily set up in our country is smashed to pieces by our army and people. And at the bottom of the scrap-heap of that machinery lie the rotten corpses of the puppet traitors. This third stage is relatively the shortest, but it is also the most victorious and valiant.

In a word, our long resistance will develop through the following stages :

a) First stage — strategy : defensive ; tactics : attack.

b) Second stage — strategy : stiff resistance (preparing for offensive) ; tactics : attack.

c) Third stage — strategy and tactics : counter-offensive.

These are the three stages of our long resistance war. In what stage are we now ? On a national scale, we are in the first stage. But, particularly in the South, where the resistance has been going on for a long time, we will switch over to the second stage soon. In fact, there are no clear dividing lines between the three stages. The later stage originates in the former. The former stage creates conditions for the later stage.

In the future, will there be any change in this three-stage war ?

There may be changes : changes in duration but not in the stages themselves. There will be no change if the French colonialists are blind and stubborn in their schemes to reoccupy Viet Nam. In the course of the war, even if the reactionary French colonialists receive support through the intervention of international reaction, the three stages in general will remain unchanged. But if we wage a powerful resistance, if the uprisings and movements for liberation in the French colonies in Africa extend and cause France many difficulties, if the movement for peaceful negotiation with Viet Nam now under way in France becomes stronger every day, if the French soldiers and legionaries in Viet Nam oppose war, and France's already faltering economy and finances become exhausted ; in short, under the pressure of these factors and in specific conditions, it is possible that the democratic parties in France may hold negotiations with us in order *to save the situation*. In that case, our long resistance will be interrupted by new talks, and that is precisely *one of its characteristics* *. However, as long as the French colonialists live in our country, and we have not yet completed the third stage, we cannot obtain genuine independence and unification.

---

* Since the beginning of the resistance (September 1945), there have been two periods of negotiations between France and Viet Nam.[40]

[40] Talks between France and the Viet-Minh took place in March, 1946, in North Viet-Nam; in July–September, 1946, in Fontainebleau, France; and briefly, in North Viet-Nam again in March, 1947. Professor Paul Mus, acting for France, crossed the front lines north of Hanoi and talked to Ho. The talks broke down over the demand that the Japanese and other foreign deserters serving as experts with the Viet-Minh forces be surrendered to the French. Another series of secret talks was to take place in Rangoon, Burma, in late 1952. On the authority of the President of France, a Vietnamese prince, Buu-Hoi (in 1963, South Viet-Nam's Ambassador to several African countries), and French legislator Jacques Raphaël-Leygues were preparing to meet Viet-Minh plenipotentiaries in Burma when the talks were called off on the basis of a U.S. promise of a sizable increase in military aid to the French forces fighting in Indochina.

XI

OUR DIFFICULTIES AND THOSE
OF THE FRENCH

The long-term resistance will be very hard, but it will certainly be victorious. That is our point of view and also the common point of view of our compatriots.

We should overcome the tendency to groundless optimism, to thinking that everything is going swimmingly with our struggle. We should do away with the tendency to under-estimation of the enemy, and over-estimation of our own forces ; such tendencies put us off our guard, leave us indifferent and unprepared, make us slacken our efforts, or cause us to lose our heads when we score the least success.

We should be fully conscious that this resistance is a hard and fierce struggle ; a long and painful trial. We must

156

have courage and patience ; we must make energetic efforts to be able to endure. We must clench our teeth and rise above ourselves to overcome all difficulties and win final victory.

Our difficulties in this resistance are many !

We have to give up a part of our territory ; thus the sphere of our action will be narrowed down, we will lose several thriving commercial cities, several major communication lines and even parts of our rich plains. How many families are thus broken up, scattered, and deprived of their means of livelihood !

Thousands of our finest youth have had to sacrifice themselves for the country ! Hundreds of talented and experienced cadres have sacrificed their lives for the fatherland ! If the war is long drawn-out there will be mountains of bones and rivers of blood. In some places, due to violent enemy raids, and our own lack of vigilance, we will suffer heavy losses in men and arms — our storehouses will be pillaged, our countryside will be dragged through blood and fire.

In the enemy-held regions, the people will suffer terrorism, rapine, destruction, pillage. Traitors and bandits will harass the people day and night and poke their noses in everywhere.

In consequence of the economic blockade, if we do not do our utmost to increase production and to establish adequate organization for the distribution of goods, we will meet difficulties in supply in some regions.

Faced with the enemy's manœuvres to divide us politically if we do not strengthen our solidarity and do our work of persuasion, there will be misunderstanding and discord between Catholics and non-Catholics, between majority and minority people, there may even be fratricidal conflicts.

Certain international reactionary forces may intervene in this war and temporarily tip the scales in favour of the French colonialists.

All this, without speaking of such natural calamities as flood and the epidemics that usually go with war !

The above-mentioned difficulties are usually met with in a war in any country. Our people must sweep them all aside, and be determined to overcome every obstacle !

The pessimists are discouraged at the least difficulty. They forget that our country is an agricultural country with rich resources, which are easily exploited ; our people are industrious and thrifty, the overhelming majority of them live by farming and will never starve through the loss of the cities (as we have said already in dealing with the resistance in the economic field.)

Our territory is relatively small. Our population is relatively small. But the enemy lives thousands of miles from our country. Moreover, he must scatter his forces to defend many places in the French Union ; thus he cannot concentrate forces to annihilate us.

Enemy terror will in fact frighten a few people, but in general it will arouse the deep hatred of our people. Indeed, the deceptive propaganda of the enemy is dangerous to us ; but then his greed and his barbarous methods straight away unmask his hypocritical face for our people to spit at in disgust. Eighty years of slavery and five years under the double yoke of the French and Japanese have driven our people to unite closely to fight to the end, and they are resolved never to live under the same sky with the invaders. For nearly two years, the people's power has brought to our people freedom and more or less important economic and cultural gains ; therefore, our people eagerly make sacrifices and are determined to preserve the gains of the republican regime.

Although we are poor in arms and munitions, thanks to guerilla tactics and their active spirit, our people can to a certain extent make good this deficiency : they can seize enemy weapons to fire them at the enemy. While fighting, they can produce still more weapons.

For nearly a century, the French invaders have never ceased to massacre the men of talent of our nation. But " young shoots replace the old bamboo ". From generation to generation, our people have fought unremittingly for independence. Men of talent have passed on the torch from one to the other. And our sacred resistance of today is forging a whole generation of heroes. If the enemy murders one of our gifted sons, certainly we will have many others to replace him.

Cowards are generally blind or have only a one-sided idea of things. They see only our difficulties, but not what we can do to overcome them. They see only our weaknesses, but not those of the enemy.

As far as the enemy is concerned, what do we see ? France is now confronted with four great difficulties :

1 — After the Second World War, French economy and finance were exhausted. France is short of coal : she must restrict the running of the machines in her factories. This year, France is short of 600,000 tons of corn, and she has not even the money to buy abroad to make good the deficiency. The regular budget and extraordinary expenditures in 1947 resulted in a deficit of 285,000 million francs. France has as yet recovered only to a small extent from

the ravages of war ; yet she must spend hundreds of millions of francs for the war in Viet Nam. This situation is having a very bad effect on the supplies to the French Expeditionary Corps.

2 — The political situation in France is confused. The de Gaulle clique are engaged in activities to set up a party, and aim to rely on foreign reaction to overthrow the republican regime. The anti-war movement has been launched. In debates on Viet Nam at the sessions of the French National Assembly in March and May, the Communist Party has clearly expressed its opposition to the policy of using force to re-establish the colonial regime in our country, and opposed the war expenditures. On March 25, 1947, the general Confederation of Labour organized throughout France many demonstrations embracing millions of people with the slogan : "Immediate negotiations with Viet Nam ".

In the future, the anti-war movement in France will certainly grow extensively.

3 — The situation in the French African colonies is in constant turmoil. On March 29, 1947, the people of Madagascar rose up to fight the French ; the insurrection is expanding day after day. On April 8, 1947, hostilities broke out between the Algerian people and the French in the Kabylia region. On the night of April 7, 1947, at Casablanca (Morocco), there were many hundreds dead and wounded in a fight between Arabs and the Senegalese soldiers of the French. In French West Africa, on April 19, 1947, railwaymen went on strike, and at the end of April the people demonstrated in front of the palace of the French Governor, etc. The movement of struggle for independence is spreading in the member countries of the French Union.

4 — The peoples in South-East Asia have shown their indignation at French aggression in Viet Nam. The Indian, Burmese, Malayan and Indonesian peoples have expressed their sympathy for us. In mid-April 1947, at a session held in India, the World Federation of Democratic Youth decided to support Viet Nam and established a program of action to demand that France cease hostilities in Viet Nam. Thus, we can see that the opinion of honest people in the world against French colonialist aggression will gradually isolate France in the international arena.

And this is only the beginning of France's difficulties. If France does not negotiate with us soon, these difficulties will grow to such an extent that France will be powerless to overcome them. Why ? Because the more France fights Viet Nam, the more she will suffer losses in manpower and material resources, the more hardships the French people will endure, the more the anti-war movement in France and the revolutionary movement in the French colonies will develop, and the more severely the democratic world will condemn French colonial policy. It is just as French Premier Ramadier said on April 27, 1947 : *"France is like a drowning man whose head is still coming up for air."*[41]

These words do not only correspond exactly to the financial and economic situation of France, but also to the her political situation. Ramadier also said :

" If we do not react, we will sink". *

---

* These words of Ramadier were designed to appeal for help from the U. S. A. and to prepare French opinion for acceptance of U. S. imperialist assistance, which will mean that France will be subservient to the U. S. But they also clearly express how critical France's situation is.

[41] This analysis of the situation in France is substantially accurate. It is an indication of the thoroughness with which the D.R.V.N. was informed— thanks to its Communist sympathizers inside France.

But in our opinion, to avoid "sinking", the only way for France is to negotiate with Viet Nam and recognize the national rights of the Vietnamese people and those of other countries in the French Union. Thus France will not fall into the arms of the American capitalists and simply be sold out to Yankees.

* * *

We have the necessary conditions to overcome all difficulties in our country. We only require that our people shall be patient, single-minded and skilful, establish plans for every task, fight strongly and increase production.

In the course of the resistance war, due to our efforts, these difficulties will diminish. These difficulties exist in our own country ; we can concentrate our forces to minimize them. Moreover, we also enjoy the assistance of our allies in the world : the French people, the peoples in the French colonies and the forces of peace, democracy and socialism headed by the Soviet Union ; thus, it is very possible for us to overcome our difficulties.

As for the French difficulties, some exist in France itself, some in Viet Nam, others in the countries of the French Union, and others in the world in general. France cannot concentrate her forces to overcome these complicated and scattered difficulties, especially as she is much weakened following the recent world war. Therefore, if France wants to be an independent and democratic country, and to keep her position as a great power in the world, she has no other way of easing or overcoming these difficulties than recognizing the independence and unification of Viet Nam. This is one more reason for the future victory of Viet Nam, and the future defeat of France.

XII

BALANCE OF FORCES

In this war as in all other wars, when two sides are fighting, the stronger will carry the day and the weaker will be defeated. Strength and weakness here mean strength and weakness in the moral and material fields, which reflect the strong and weak points of each side. Whichever side has more strong points and less weak points will be able to triumph over the other.

It is difficult for the side which has many strong points, but in minor matters, and few weaknesses, but in major matters, to defeat the other side which has fewer strong points, but in major matters, and more weaknesses, but in minor matters. The side whose strong points grow and weaknesses diminish as the fighting wears on will be able to defeat the other side, whose strong points diminish and whose weaknesses grow with the fighting.

Therefore, to know which side — our people or the French — will win or lose, we have to consider objectively the strong points and the weaknesses of the two sides.

Here are our strong points :

a) The aim of our war is just (we are struggling against aggressors in order to recover our freedom).

b) The entire people are united (in the National United Front to fight the French invaders).

c) The morale of our army and people is high (everyone eagerly and heroically struggles for national salvation).

d) Our troops fight on their native soil to defend their people's interests, and they thus enjoy three advantages : they are used to the climate (Thien thoi * the climate is favourable to them), well acquainted with the natural features (Dia loi * the terrain is favourable to them) and supported by the people (Nhan hoa * the population is favourable to them).

e) We have many allies (the French people, the peoples of the French colonies, the forces of peace, democracy and socialism the world over, support us).

Our weaknesses stand as follows :

a) Our weapons are few and rudimentary.

b) Our troops are not numerous and not yet inured to war.

c) Our organizational level is low (particularly in the military and economic fields).

---

* These are the three classic principles of **Sun Tsu**, a great **Chinese strategist.**

d) Propaganda directed to foreign countries is weak.

Here are the weaknesses of the enemy :

a) The aim of their war is reactionary (aggression, oppression, exploitation, which arouse hatred for them).

b) Internal division (the backers of the war, the supporters of peace, the reactionary forces and the progressive forces, sharply oppose one another).

c) The low morale of their troops (several facts show that the French soldiers are afraid of death ; puppet soldiers, legionaries and French colonial soldiers have come over to our ranks).

d) Waging an aggressive war in a foreign country, the enemy meets with three disadvantages : not used to the climate (lack of a climate favourable to them), not acquainted with the natural features (lack of a terrain favourable to them) * not supported by the people (lack of a population favourable to them).

e) They enjoy little assistance, but are confronted by many enemies (the British and American imperialists may back them to a certain extent, in weapons, finance, etc., but this is merely a drop in the bucket compared with their huge expenditures, because France must heal the wounds of war at home and at the same time meet the expenditures in Indochina, face up to the struggle of the colonial peoples in Africa, and even the anti-war movement in France).

f) Finance and economy are in a state of exhaustion (France has not yet been restored after the Second World War, and now has to fight against Viet Nam and Madagascar.

---

* Though the French invaders have lived for 80 years in our country, they cannot be so well acquainted with our land as our own people.

That is why her already poor finances and economy are becoming poorer).

g) Their forces are limited and must be scattered throughout the French Union.

Here are the French strong points :

a) Numerous modern arms,

b) Numerous well-trained troops,

c) High level of organization,

d) Large-scale propaganda directed to foreign countries.

Comparing the advantages and the disadvantages of the two sides, we notice the five following points.

Firstly, the advantages of Viet Nam are the disadvantages of the French, and *vice versa*.

Secondly, France has more weaknesses than Viet Nam.

Third, France has more weaknesses than strong points.

Fourth, Most of the strong points of Viet Nam are political ones ; most of the French strong points are military ones.

Fifth, All the strong points of Viet Nam are fundamental ; and those of the French are *auxiliary*. Indeed, the French have many modern arms, numerous and well-trained officers and troops, a high standard of organization and large-scale propaganda with foreign countries ; but their war is an aggressive war, so they have few friends and many enemies, suffer from internal division, and cannot enjoy the support of the people ; their effective strength is constantly diminished.[42]

Thus, their strong points are rendered useless.

The experience of wars in history, and particularly the new experiences of the Second World War, have shown

[42] The last two paragraphs again show the emphasis the Viet-Minh leadership places on *political* rather than *military* factors—a principle to which the Western side pays assiduous lip service but which it fails to follow in practice.

this clearly. How were affairs with the Germany of Hitler, with fascist Japan ? Had they not many modern arms, able generals and well-trained troops, good organization and clever propaganda ? Yet, because of the aggressive and reactionary aims of their war, their army and people were not single-minded. The morale of their troops was very low. They were opposed by the whole civilized world. They could only win some resounding victories at the beginning. After that, the more they fought the weaker they became until they were smashed to bits and overthrown. The French colonialists must learn this historic lesson, go back quickly on their error, or France's future will be very gloomy.

We should keep well in mind that if we protract the war, thanks to the strenuous efforts of our entire people, our strong points will constantly increase, and our weaknesses will decrease with every passing day. On the contrary, the more the enemy fights, the less his strong points, the more his weaknesses. Here are some easily grasped examples : The more we fight, the more our troops are inured to war, experienced and tempered. The more the enemy fights the more critical his financial and economic situation. The more we fight, the more we enjoy the support and sympathy of the French people and peace-loving peoples the world over, the more the peoples of the French colonies will avail themselves of the sending of French troops to Viet Nam to rise up against the French, the more numerous our allies. The more the French fight, the lower their morale, the more weary and demoralized their forces.

So we see that the more we fight, the stronger our forces, the more the enemy fights the weaker his forces.

Though at present our material strength (weapons, troops, economy, etc.) is still inferior to that of the enemy, our moral strength (the heroism and solidarity of our army and people, the moral support given by the world's people) is tremendous. In the future, if we prolong the war, not only will our moral strength develop, but our material forces will also increase. Our protracted war aims at developing every reserve of material and moral power, strengthening our strong points, minimising the weak ones, in order to be able to switch over from a weak position to a stronger position than the enemy to win final victory.

In a word, after comparing our forces with the enemy's, we can affirm that *we will certainly win*. Our resistance war is a people's war, a progressive war. We enjoy the material and moral strength drawn from the inexhaustible resources of the people, from the progressive character of a just war. Temporary failures cannot discourage us, just as small and partial successes cannot intoxicate us. We know that at any time and anywhere, revolutionary success can be obtained only if we organize and make preparations to win it. Our success in this resistance war will be partly owing to the difficulties, weaknesses and errors of the French (which we know how to exploit to the fullest extent), and partly thanks to the assistance of our allies ; but it will be *chiefly due to our close unity, our self-reliance, our strenuous efforts to strenghten and develop our forces. Long-term resistance and self-reliance are our general guiding principle in this war for national liberation.*

The three great points which will lead us to success are :

1. The entire Vietnamese people are closely united to wage a long resistance war.

2. The French people will more strongly oppose war day after day, or will rise up to overthrow the reactionaries.

3. The revolutionary movement in the French colonies is on the upgrade and the forces of peace and democracy all over the world struggle energetically to oppose the French colonialists.

These three factors already exist, but they are not yet ripe. We should make still more sacrifices and struggle with all our might. Time will bring us more favourable opportunities.

At present, the French reactionaries are plotting a mischievous manœuvre, hoping to overcome all their difficulties and make good the weaknesses of France.

They intend to go in for anti-Soviet propaganda, and anti-Communism ; they seek to undermine the Republic, to crush the French people under the burden of war spending and push France into the arms of the U.S. and Britain in the hope of winning help from these powers to restore the French economy and to prolong the colonial war. But for France this path is suicidal, because France will thus turn herself into a country subservient to foreign powers and, finally, will be unable even to maintain the French Union. The French people and all parties loyal to the French Republic will assuredly not stand by with folded arms in the face of these mischievous activities of the French reactionaries. They will rise up in struggle. At that moment, their struggle will combine with that of the Vietnamese resistance war, and with the struggle of other peoples in the French Union, and will switch over to a co-ordinated offensive which will defeat the French reactionaries.

XIII

WHAT MUST BE DONE

We have described our strong and weak points, and the strong and weak points of the enemy. But this exposition does not exhaust the question of victory or defeat in the war.

We should not be content with comparing the potentialities and problems, the strengths and weaknesses of the two sides, and slip into complacency because of our advantages. The attitude of groundless optimism robs us of clear vision, makes us short-sighted, passive, and without the will to make progress.

In the history of war, there have been countries which met with fewer difficulties and had fewer weaknesses than the enemy, but which failed. On the other hand, there have been countries which met with more difficulties and had more weaknesses than the enemy, but which triumphed. Why should this be so ? Because the country which had the advantage of its enemy did not try hard enough, underestimated its enemy and lacked skill. On the other hand, the country whose situation was disadvantageous made strenuous efforts, "knew itself and knew the enemy", and triumphed because it had skilful leadership. The author of " Kim Van Kieu " * when he wrote : " The will of man triumphs over fate ", was thinking of the talent and subjective efforts of man, which may exercise a great influence on objective conditions. Of course, if we look at this question closely, we can see that this influence is more or less powerful depending on the favourable or unfavourable objective material conditions.

When our people struggle, when our leadership is skilful, we can take advantage of the favourable conditions of time and situation to turn " difficulties " into " advantages ", " weaknesses " into " strengths ", and there is nothing strange in this at all ! Moreover, war itself is a great movement. Difficulties for the belligerents created by the war (" strengths " or " weaknesses " depending on the side), cannot remain unchanged. They change according to the development of the war. The side which is skilful and makes great efforts will be able to cause these changes to be of advantage to itself, and harmful to the enemy. On the other hand, if this side lacks vigilance, is foolish, passive, or cowardly, these changes will become advantageous to enemy and harmful to it.

---

* Poem written by Nguyen Du (18th century), acknowledged as the masterpiece of Vietnamese literature.

Moreover, we should ask ourselves : if we have more strong points than the enemy, then why do we remain on the defensive and go on retreating ? Why, looking at our situation in general, do we still remain in a passive position, and have not yet won the initiative ? In our opinion, it is because most of the enemy's weaknesses are moral ones, and most of his strong points are material ones. As for us, our weaknesses are for the most part material, and our strong points moral. War is a struggle between two forces from both moral and material viewpoints. Material conditions are quite necessary to victory-even a temporary victory-in any military action, whether in war, or in an armed uprising.

That it why, to check the advance of the enemy, to defeat him, we should strive to diminish our material weaknesses, increase our moral strength, and at the same time reduce the material strong points of the enemy and aggravate his moral weaknesses.

Herein lies the question.

Because we have fewer arms than the enemy, while fighting we must on the one hand maintain and develop our arsenals, keep up and increase our flow of weapons ; and on the other hand, we must destroy and capture enemy arms to a greater and greater extent. It is a pity that our firepower is still weak and that our tactics are not yet skilful : in many battles, though we have killed a considerable number of enemy soldiers, we have seized only a very small quantity of weapons. On the other hand, though we have suffered small losses in men, every time one of our fighters falls, we lose his weapon as well. While fighting we must also produce arms, both rudimentary and modern arms,

and constantly improve the standard of our arms manufac-
ture. We should overcome the tendency to overestimate
modern arms and underestimate the rudimentary. Those
who have these tendencies do not realise that with the
technical conditions prevailing in our country, if the manu-
facture of rudimentary arms is not carried on, we cannot
arm our guerilla forces and our entire people.

But at the same time we should overcome the tendency
to attach importance only to rudimentary arms and not
strive to produce the modern ; if we lack modern arms, it
is difficult to check the advance of the enemy's motorized
troops, or to counter - attack him. On the other hand we
should carry out sabotage, intercept the enemy and use
guerilla warfare with a view to minimizing the effect of the
enemy's modern arms. We should launch surprise attacks
and blow up enemy munitions stores, set up sham targets,
which are exposed and easily visible, in order to delude the
enemy and inveigle him into firing, expending his ammu-
nition to no effect.

Our troops are not as inured to war as those of the
enemy ; that is why, while fighting, we must learn rapidly
from the experiences accumulated in every battle and study
the enemy's tactics, improve our own strategy and tactics,
strive to train our officers and soldiers, militia and guerilla
forces. At the same time, we use strategems to deceive the
enemy and drive him on to the defensive ; we find out as
much as possible about the enemy in order to get to know him ;
we keep him in the dark about our forces by depriving him
of information ; we should clearly foresee the enemy's plans,
taking advantage of his carelessness and lack of vigilance to

launch daring attacks to annihilate him, avoiding all disadvantageous « fights to the death » to conserve our forces for a long resistance, for the moment when we can switch over from a defensive to an offensive position.

At present, most of our armymen know only how to fight bravely ; they do not pay attention to the study of tactics. Many officers are often concerned only with routine, knowing only the area in which they are fighting, not bothering to study and analyse matters thoroughly ; or they collect experiences mechanically, and do not know how to apply them correctly to our practical situation ; they limit themselves to positional warfare or to the former strategy and tactics of the colonialist army. These tendencies should be weeded out immediately.

Our level of war organisation is low ; therefore we should urgently try to discover every means of improving our command, which must be unified, rapid and precise. It is necessary to simplify and militarize the various technical organs. We should give precise orders, which must reach every fighter, and strictly control the implementation of these orders. Liaison and communications must be rapid and consolidated, even in enemy-held regions. All information must be speedy and accurate. Supplies should be punctual, sufficient and regular. Militia and guerilla forces must be widely organised with a view to replenishing our reserve forces constantly, so that we can reinforce the regular army in such a way that our regular armymen receive timely relief and do not wear themselves out. At the same time, we must strive to upset the enemy's organisation by sabotage and ruses. If, to achieve the aims of the resistance war, our line and policies must be correct, and our strategy and tatics flexible and clever, organisational work, too, is very necessary, in order to ensure the implementation of lines and policies, and the correct application of strategy and tactics. We should overcome the tendency to work in an amateurish manner, according to the way we feel, without principle, in a routine fashion, without order, without planning and checking. We should at the same time struggle against the tendency to waste time and effort over trifles, not to see the question as a whole ; or the tendency to do poor organisational work which is incapable of ensuring the execution of the political line.

Is our propaganda directed to foreign countries weak ? We will do our utmost to explain our just cause and expose the enemy's schemes before the world.

We uphold a just cause against barbarism, employ sincerity against perfidy. Therefore, we shall certainly win the sympathy of the French people, of personalities in other countries, of small nations, particularly Asian people and the peoples of the French colonies. Furthermore, we might request the Soviet Union to raise the problem of Viet Nam before the United Nations Organisation and demand that France negotiate with Viet Nam. We should take full advantage of the contradictions between France and other countries to make propaganda against the French colonialists. That is why we must collect documents concerning French crimes against our people, against foreign residents and the adherents of various religions ; and documents proving our humanitarian behaviour towards French prisoners of war, our correct policies in regard to all religious people and foreign residents. Propaganda with foreign countries must be undertaken by a responsible organ, and by a number of specialized cadres, in order to avoid negligence and a happy-go-lucky manner of working. We should also send abroad cultural delegates or National Assembly deputies to make propaganda. We should get rid of the tendency to consider propaganda with foreign countries as a completely auxiliary task and thus neglect it ; or to consider it as a " panacea ", or, in other words, to rely upon others without making any attempt to develop our own resources, or to make our own efforts.

Such are the things to be done to minimize our weaknesses and diminish the enemy's strong points. To develop our strong points and accentuate the enemy's weaknesses, there is no other way than to carry out the following fundamental tasks : to unite the entire people, mobilize the whole country, wage a long resistance, make skilful propaganda with the enemy and have a good foreign policy.

However, if we know how to direct our subjective efforts to turning his disadvantages against the enemy, is the enemy so stupid as not to aim our own disadvantages at our heads in return ? The enemy is more perfidious and cunning than we think.

In the course of the resistance war, some disadvantages may come our way, created by efforts made by the enemy, by our own errors, or by circumstances unforeseen either by us or the enemy. For instance : natural calamities, or famine might occur, there might be intervention by a third country which would first help the French colonialists to fight us and then oust them ; again, the loss of a number of our cadres and outstanding men could have a considerable effect on the leadership of the resistance ; or grave errors by our officers could lead to serious losses...

Such things may happen. The duty of our leading organization * is to foresee such eventualities and take all necessary preventive measures. But when something has happened that we were unable to prevent, we should remain calm, hold out, and deal with the situation. If we stick closely to the people, we will never be defeated.

---

* The leading organization here is the Indochinese Communist Party (now the Viet Nam Lao Dong Party). In this book, the author does not refer by name to the Indochinese Communist Party, the Party having proclaimed its voluntary dissolution. In truth it continued its activities. (Editor's note). [43]

[43] It is significant that the editor candidly admits that the "dissolution" of the ICP in 1945 was simply a camouflage and that the Party continued its activities underground until it reappeared in the open in 1951.

XIV

SOME BURNING PROBLEMS IN THE MILITARY FIELD

The nation-wide resistance war has been waged for nearly six months. The war is expanding and becoming fiercer every day. Here is a brief summary of the main points concerning a number of burning military questions :

1. *Politics and military action* — These two questions are closely related : *"War is a continuation of politics."* (Marx). The politics of our Democratic Republic are hampered by the French colonialists ; we must therefore act militarily to overcome the obstacles they have put in our way, so that our politics can be carried out successfully. Military action is a measure by which politics are executed. " War is a means of politics. *War is the continuation of*

politics by other means." (Clausewitz). This is why military action can only succeed when politics are correct. And conversely, politics cannot be fulfilled without the success of military action. When military action is successful the aim of war is also realized. After a war comes to an end, politics continue to be carried out by other, more moderate means. That is the relation between military affairs and politics.

Those who rely only on politics often do not realize the important role of armed force in history, do not realize that sometimes armed force must be used to fight the internal enemy or external aggressors. Internally, such people often accept reconciliation contrary to principle. In foreign relations, they are liable to surrender, or make diplomatic concesssions. Again, those who have a tendency only to rely on military action are inclined to militarism. They tend to believe that everything can be settled by armed force ; they do not apply political mobilization, are unwilling to give explanations and to convince people ; they even use threats, or bring pressure to bear on the people. Or, fighting spiritedly, they neglect political work ; they do not seek ways of building ties of affection between officers and men, do not act in such a way that the army and the people can wholeheartedly help one another ; and they neglect propaganda directed to the breaking of the morale of the enemy troops. Such people know only how to fight ; they fail to consolidate the National United Front, fail to seek new allies outside the country, and neglect the study of the internal and world situation, which is indispensable to the development of correct internal and foreign policies.[44]

---

[44] This paragraph is perhaps the most important in the whole book, for it points directly to the present deficiencies in Western operations in South Viêt-Nam, with their overemphasis on military technology and their lack of a valid political rationale, e.g., strategic hamlets are a technique, not an ideology.

2. *Strategy and tactics* — In brief, strategy is the art of war directed to winning victory in a given war. Tactics is the art of fighting to defeat the enemy in a given battle. Tactics is an integral part of strategy. To succeed, strategy must first of all be correct. If strategy is correct but tactics happen to be wrong, the war will not necessarily fail entirely. On the other hand, tactics may well be correct, but if strategy is wrong, in the long run tactics will be of no use. (This was obvious in the Soviet-German and Sino-Japanese wars.) Nevertheless, if strategy is correct and tactics are consistently wrong, the numerous errors in tactics may lead to strategic failure. Or sometimes a very great tactical error may also have a harmful effect on strategy. After all, though a strategy may be correct, if command is weak and suffers continual losses in all battles, how can strategy succeed ? Again, due to a single heavy defeat, which shatters the army's strength and destroys the morale of the troops, strategy may be confronted with danger. (For example, the defeats suffered by the Germans in the battle of Verdun in the First World War, and in the battle of Stalingrad during the Second World War).

Moreover, strategy decides tactics. Our strategy is to protract the war ; therefore, in tactics, we should avoid unfavourable fights to the death, because we must maintain our forces.

3. *Defence and attack* — At present, we are strategically in the stage of contention. But it is wrong if, on the pretext of defence and preservation of forces, we keep on retreating and do not fight. The Thai Binh battle of April 11, 1947 showed the confusion of the local command in this connection, a confusion which caused sorrow and shame to the troops who were indignant at not being

allowed to fight, and discouraged the people who felt mistrust for the army and lost confidence.

Sometimes it is better to fight a more or less losing battle than to retreat with unimpaired forces and leave behind a very bad impression. Sometimes we must use forces smaller than those of the enemy to defend a very important position at the peril of our lives, awaiting the arrival of our main forces, who will be able to annihilate the whole initially superior enemy force.

We should bear in mind that in this stage our strategy is defence, but our tactics are those of constant attack. This means that in the whole country we still remain on the defensive, but in each battle we attack and annihilate the enemy. In strategy, the war must be prolonged, but in tactics, lightning attacks must be launched and rapid decisions won. In other words, *" prolonging the defence in the rear "*, and *" attacking to decide rapidly at the front "*. *

In general, our cadres already understand this point. But there are still some who do not understand it thoroughly ; that is the reason why there is this tendency to give up fighting and run away.

Moreover, we are used to remaining on the defensive in positional warfare, but not yet used to applying mobile warfare in defence, or to launching attacks to ensure defence. So, when we want to defend a position, we often have the tendency to establish a fixed line of defence, dig trenches, set up fortifications and defend them in a rigid manner ; we do not know how to combine guerilla and mobile tactics to attack and encircle the enemy, cut off his supply lines, attack him on the flank or from behind, with

---

* Mao Tse-tung : " On the Protracted War ".

the aim of obliging him to withdraw; nor do we always know when to send our troops to attack a position important to the enemy to oblige him to detach a part of his attacking forces to save this position. By such means, our defence is reinforced in the area in which we are under attack. The attack launched by our forces on Haiphong on March 21, 1947 obliged the enemy to send a part of his forces from Hongay and Quang Yen to Haiphong, thus reinforcing our defence in these places, at which we were under attack. The Loc Binh battle at the end of March 1947 obliged the enemy to despatch forces from An Chau to defend the Lang Son-Tien Yen road, thus increasing our strength for the defence of Luc Nam. These are examples of active defence, of defence by offence.

4. Wearing down and annihilation — To wage war is to fight in such a way as to annihilate the enemy forces in battles, and at the same time to increase our own forces with a view to the final defeat of the enemy. So we must apply the tactics of wearing down (to wear away the enemy and exhaust him) and annihilating (to kill or capture the enemy.)

At present, the enemy forces are still stronger than ours. That is why we must protract the war to wear them down. Only by wearing the enemy down, can we fulfil the strategic tasks of launching the general counter-offensive, annihilating the enemy and winning final victory. But must we wait for the stage of general counter offensive to annihilate the enemy ? Clearly, no. During the two first stages themselves (contention and equilibrium) we must also launch attacks to annihilate the enemy forces partially, to wear them down *as much as possible*, and seize their weapons, munitions, etc., to provide our forces with more arms.

This is the most active way to work towards the moment of general counter-offensive in which the enemy as a whole will be annihilated.

Up to now our troops have often launched attacks to wear the enemy down ; in these attacks, both sides have suffered losses, though ours have been smaller than the enemy's. From now on, battles of annihilation must be applied to a greater extent than battles of wearing down. What is mobile warfare if it is not the tactics of annihilation ? And guerilla warfare, if it is not a combination of the tactics of wearing down and of annihilation ? * Our regular army must often apply mobile warfare in order partially to annihilate enemy forces. As for the guerilla forces, they must harass and decimate the enemy, and at the same time launch sudden attacks and stage ambushes to achieve rapid annihilation of the enemy forces involved.

5. How should we attack ? — Attack is the only effective means of annihilation of the enemy. Fighting the enemy without attacking him is not fighting. However, most of our troops — both militia and guerilla forces — do not yet clearly understand how to attack. They often split up their forces to contest a series of enemy positions simultaneously, and call this kind of action an " attack ". They go and attack some position without reconnoitring, without planning, and are shouting " Assault " two hundred yards before they reach the enemy, giving him plenty of time to get ready to receive them...This they also call an " attack ".

---

* The main characteristic of mobile warfare is annihilating ; the main characteristic of positional warfare is wearing down ; the main characteristics of guerilla warfare are annihilating and wearing down.

No ! In our opinion to attack — for example a city or an enemy post — we must :

a) Make careful inquiries into the enemy's position, his forces, his weapons, his morale, the character of the commander, etc., with a view to drawing up a detailed plan, and then secretly make careful preparations. (But we should avoid formalism and slowness, which could cause us to miss good opportunities).

b) Concentrate forces superior to those of the enemy and such as will enable us to annihilate him in one battle. *Concentration is an essential law of attack.* (Use our regular army, when it is superior to that of the enemy, to launch a sudden attack on the objective ; never use more than half of our forces for defensive purposes, or to pin down the enemy in some auxiliary area. Of course while we remain on the defensive, the regular army must be quartered in some place, playing the role of a reserve force, awaiting an opportunity to launch a successful attack. But when we are on the offensive, we must use the regular army for sudden attacks, not utilising it as a reserve force only. This is the one way in which we can rapidly annihilate the enemy.)

c) *Attack in an active, rapid, alert manner, adapt oneself speedily to the new situation* — When the attack is decided upon, and once the order is given, officers and men must be courageous, bold, and attack very rapidly. The troops must be divided for the advance and regrouped to attack, encircle, work round the enemy positions and finally take them by storm.

d) Define the principal direction clearly.

We should concentrate our forces to defeat the enemy at one point in a sudden attack ; attack the most important key-positions of the enemy, completely paralysing his power of defence. It is possible to divide our forces to engage the enemy in one direction, while we actually plan to attack him in another direction entirely.

e) Launch lightning, surprise attacks *availing oursel-ves of moments when the enemy is off his guard*, when he is eating or sleeping, or when it is drizzling or dark, to attack vigorously for a rapid annihilation of the enemy.

f) Hold any position taken in an attack, or, if we do not intend to hold it, retreat immediately in order to preser-ve our forces for new battles. We should not always hold the position seized, because the enemy may assemble stronger forces to launch a counter-offensive, seize back the position and destroy our forces. But, in case of withdrawal, if the conditions are favourable to us, we should profit by our victory to mop up the front and complete the destruc-tion of enemy forces.

g) *Make full and thorough use of the victorious attack* to enhance the prestige of our troops and the morale of our whole army and people. Experiences must be drawn from all attacks for the preparation of others.

In a word, attack is an art. To attack successfully, we must know the enemy and we must know our own forces. We must study the conditions of time and place, rapidly concentrate sufficient forces, and attack in an active, alert and rapid manner.

6. *How do we win the initiative ?* — At present, the enemy is the stronger and we are the weaker. That is why, looking at the situation as a whole, the enemy remains on the offensive and we on the defensive. But being on the defensive, we must win the initiative. *To keep the initiative is the essential principle of tactics in general, and of guerilla and mobile warfare in particular.*

There are many ways of winning the initiative :

a) *To lure the enemy*, by diverse means, to make him fall into a trap prepared by us. This is one way in which, though weaker than the enemy, we can nevertheless keep the initiative. Sometimes, even though our forces are not numerous, and our weapons not modern, we may cleverly lure the enemy into our trap in order to annihilate him. For example, we can worry him on the left before attacking suddenly on the right, in such a way that the enemy does not know where the attack is coming from and so is unable to ward off the blow.

b) *To attack the enemy's exposed and weak points* in order to make it impossible for him to defend himself. We can take advantage of moments when the enemy is least expecting it to attack him. For instance : when the enemy moves, we lay in ambush to attack him ; when the enemy troops, worn out by a long march, arrive at their destination we launch a sudden attack on them.

c) To mobilize the entire people to rise up and *wage guerilla warfare everywhere in order to scatter and wear down the enemy, and to enable our regular forces to launch sudden attacks to annihilate him in determined positions ;* to organize the people, to hush up all news, to conceal our troops, so that the enemy has no notion of our activities and we have favourable conditions for our sudden attacks.

d) *To move skilfully*, advancing rapidly towards the enemy rear, attacking important points, with a view to obliging the enemy troops to regroup, thus upsetting their predetermined battle plan ; to strike the enemy on his flank and from behind, rather than throwing ourselves directly at his main front.

e) To clearly know the enemy's situation in order to be able to *concentrate our regular troops rapidly and move our reserve forces swiftly to the required areas to act in good time*. (At present, our forces are not only weak in intelligence work but also slow in moving and regrouping ; they often cannot use or do not know how to use their reserves).

f) To centralize the leadership in the hands of a higher command. But the local commands *can and must act according to the situation at the front*, and must fight according to their own initiative in order not to miss good opportunities or to fall into a state of passivity. (In many places, conditions have been favourable, but the commands, on the pretext that they had received no orders, refused to fight ; thus, they tied their own hands and failed to act, often creating a dangerous situation.)

Such are the general measures required to win the initiative. On the one hand, we should not fight unfavourable battles, or fight without preparation ; we should not allow ourselves to be forced by the enemy to fight in unfavourable conditions. On the other hand, we should have the initiative, not let slip good opportunities, strive to make full use of guerilla and mobile warfare, actively attack the enemy at his weak points, attack when the enemy is careless, and cleverly use ruses to lure the enemy into our traps.

When facing more powerful enemy forces, if the guerilla forces want to keep the initiative while fighting, they must follow the four rules drawn up by Comrade Mao Tse-tung :

a) When the enemy advances, we retreat ;

b) When the enemy halts, we harass him ;

c) When the enemy is worn out, we attack him ;

d) When the enemy runs away, we pursue him;

There may exist some further rules :

— When the enemy concentrates, we disperse ;

— We may lure the enemy deep into our positions, etc.

7. *Resistance bases* — A resistance base is an area in which it is relatively safe for us to train our regular army, train cadres, produce arms and munitions, tend our wounded, etc.

There are many kinds of bases : mountainous areas, in the delta and in marshy areas.

Areas fit for the establishment of such bases are those where :

a) The people are active, widely organized and ready to support the army in every field.

b) There are regular troops ready to make sacrifices and hurl themselves forward to stay the enemy's advance, to safeguard the base and defend the leading organs and the population.

c) The natural features of the country are favourable to our defence.

Of the above three conditions, the first two are of course the more important. Where there are neither forests nor mountains, if we have regular forces with a high morale and broad masses who are politically conscious, these will constitute human forests and mountains to protect us.

There are people who think that because our territory is small, it is impossible for us to establish resistance bases. Such a conception is wrong. It comes from an overestimation of the enemy's forces. Though our territory is small it is not so small that it is impossible to set up resistance bases in it. Moreover, the enemy forces are limited, they come from afar. It is certain that they cannot wipe out and annihilate our forces, and they have not sufficient forces to occupy our whole territory and prevent us from getting a foothold.

Others consider that a resistance base is an absolutely safe area where we can carry out construction on a large and permanent scale. This viewpoint is also wrong. It comes from the over-estimation of our own forces. No base can be absolutely firm! That is why we must not and cannot build anything that, while it may be imposing, is cumbersome and difficult to move in case of need.

When we occupy a place, we must have always in mind the moment when we may have to leave it. When we defend a place, we must always have in mind the moment when we may have to abandon it. However, we should not make the mistake of thinking of a base as merely a place where we quarter our troops. The " one day base " of which the comrades in Quang Tri have often spoken was only a temporary cantonment, no more and no less.

When we choose an area as a base we should convene a conference of high-level cadres of the army, the administration and of the people's organizations of the region to discuss the establishment and defence of the base. The following questions require prime attention :

1. In mass work, we should develop and consolidate the mass organizations (prepare underground groups), and train local cadres to maintain and lead the mass organizations in the region.

2. In military affairs, we should widely establish militia forces and arm the entire people, giving the young people military training ; we should dispose the regular forces and weapons necessary to check the advance of the

enemy and to destroy his forces once they have penetrated deep into our base area ; we should conceal military objectives, and endeavour to prevent enemy planes from causing us harm.

3. As for the people's well-being, production should be increased according to a determined plan ; supply must be organized and the people's living conditions improved.

4. Concerning security, we should wipe out traitors to the nation, restrict and control the circulation of persons, and deprive the enemy of all news.

* * *

Such are the urgent military problems set for us by the war. All cadres, the army and the people, and especially the military commanders at all levels, must have a clear understanding of these questions so that existing shortcomings may be speedily done away with and all errors harmful to the struggle corrected.

To defeat the enemy, strenuous efforts must be made, as has already been stated above. Making good deficiencies and correcting errors in our command require an especially great subjective effort on our part.

XV

LAUNCHING THE MILITIA MOVEMENT[45]

As has been said, our war is a people's war. The people's war must be waged by the people themselves. This means that not only does the regular army fight the enemy, but all those who are enthusiastic — regardless of sex, or of whether they are in the army or not — also take part in the fighting. Born of the people, the army defends the people and enjoys the people's support. For that reason, our fighters have a very high morale. A war waged by both the army and the people is one whose tactics are very alert and varied, conforming to the topography and the possibilities for fighting in every locality (tactics of guerilla warfare and mobile warfare). Furthermore, the war can be protracted until our final victory, despite the barbarity of the enemy forces and all their modern weapons.

[45] This chapter, although written in 1947, also has great validity for the present; it constitutes a key element in the Viet-Minh's doctrine concerning the organization of "base areas."

How is the people's war to be carried out ? We must arm the people, *launch the militia movement.* To launch the militia movement is the best means of mobilizing the entire people to take part in the fighting ; it is a measure aimed at organising and training a numerous reserve army to serve the regular army and to enable the latter to prolong the war.

The enemy troops massacre people, occupy our land, plunder our property, rape our women and destroy our crops. All those in the localities who are courageous and healthy, rise up, arms in hand, to defend the lives and property of the population. By self-defence, they help the people to carry on their work and production, help them to carry out the policy of scorched earth, seek information, suppress traitors, and carry out sabotage when need be. At the same time, they do not abandon their ordinary work. They love their native soil, their Fatherland. They are deeply attached to their villages, their ricefields and the graves of their ancestors. Highly indignant at the overbearing and vile acts of the enemy, they take up knives, sticks, spears, cross-bows, guns, grenades, mines, sometimes even a bamboo spear or a stone or a brick, to kill the enemy. They help the regular troops or the local guerilla forces to fight the enemy. These are the self-defence militia forces.

A portion of the most enthusiastic and thorough-going of them will leave their ordinary work to form themselves into a guerilla group, or, together with elements of the regular forces, organize local guerilla groups. These groups do not participate in production any longer and move about in a specific region. Their duties consist of defending a region or a district against the terrorist mopping-up activity of the enemy, supporting the people in their farming work, opposing the enemy's plunder of people's property, carrying out armed propaganda, repressing traitors and bandits, laying ambushes to attack the enemy, and launching sudden attacks on his isolated posts. At the same time, they constantly co-ordinate their action with the regular forces to wear down, attack and destroy enemy forces. Their weapons are relatively better than those of the self-defence militia forces. They should comprise guns, machine-guns, mines, grenades, bazookas, etc.

Self-defence militia, guerilla and regular forces are the three forms of our people's armed struggle at the present time *. The entire people and the militia and guerilla forces back up the regular troops. The militia forces from many villages, from many districts, gathered together to fight the enemy, can form a local guerilla detachment. The advanced local guerilla detachments which gather together to fight the enemy can become regular troops. In the course of our long-term resistance, from ordinary civilian to regular soldier, there is an endless process of development. We see that the people constitute the source of manpower for the army ; and from the militia and guerilla forces we recruit and train our regular forces. If the guerilla forces are strong, the regular forces will be strong. If the militia, guerilla and

---

* At present, in the first stage, our armed organizations are divided only into two categories : regular army and militia; the militia is in turn divided into two categories : guerilla militia and self-defence militia. But in the future, when our arms and military cadres become more numerous, we will have a clear-cut distinction of three categories : regular forces, local guerilla forces and militia forces. The militia forces do not give up production : as for the local guerilla forces, they do not take part in production, since they must move about and seek out the enemy fight to him.

regular forces are strong, we will certainly triumph. Lenin has said :

" *Victory will belong to the side which has many reserve troops, and plenty of vitality and endurance drawn from the masses.* " *

Does our militia movement now exist ? Certainly it does ; but it is not yet widespread, is not yet the nation-wide ferment that it must become. In regions such as South Viet Nam, the southern part of Central Viet Nam, and, recently, the provinces of Thua Thien and Quang Tri, and around Hanoi, Haiphong, and Nam Dinh, the militia movement has developed and is surging forward.

Generally speaking, the training and arming of our militia and guerilla forces is going ahead at a satisfactory rate. Good points of our militia and guerilla men are their activity and initiative. The battles waged by the militia and guerillas on Road No. 5, around the capital, on the road from Saigon to Mytho, at Ban Long (Quang Tri province) at the beginning of this year, in Dinh Bang (Bac Ninh province), and at Cu Da (Hadong province) last month, are worthy examples for the whole country. The organization of fortified villages and underground defence works by our militia and guerilla forces in many places is highly praiseworthy. Several special groups have been formed with a view to attacking tanks, waging battles on the rivers, or using mines against the enemy. Nevertheless, the militia movement still has many shortcomings and makes many errors. It is not yet unified, it is still formalistic, it is not yet properly in its stride. It lacks arms, particularly bullets, grenades and mines, which are

---

* Speech read at the Eighth Congress of the All-Russian Soviets.

very necessary to guerilla forces. It is short of training and leading cadres ; its political work is weak : in some places, there is even resentment among the people against the militia and guerilla men. Misunderstandings and petty jealousies between guerilla and regular forces are not yet wiped out ; co-operation with the regular troops in battle is not yet close. Some militia men in the villages tend to let their daily work slip ; some guerilla troops tend to fight rigidly in the manner of positional warfare, and have not yet learnt to apply guerilla tactics skilfully.

We hope that the comrades responsible for our militia and guerilla forces will do their best to develop the militia and guerilla movement everywhere, and launch a *patriotic competition movement to organize militia forces* and fortified villages, between cantons, districts and provinces and even in enemy-held regions. We hope that these comrades will strive to arm the militia forces, make them understand that they should exchange *their rudimentary weapons for modern ones taken from the enemy*, and disseminate battle experiences of the militia and guerillas among the guerilla forces in the enemy-held areas so that the enemy's rear can be harassed without let-up. We hope that the regular forces, as well as the militia and guerilla forces, will do their utmost to do away with all unreasonable jealousies. The regular forces, the militia and the guerilla forces are brothers. They are born of the same mother, the people. The regular forces should train militia and guerilla forces at their places of cantonment. The militia and guerilla forces should support and welcome the regular forces whenever they appear. When regular troops withdraw, they must inform the militia and guerilla forces of the fact beforehand. The militia and guerilla men who go to seek out the enemy to fight him must inform the regular troops of what they are doing and co-operate with them in fighting if need be. When they capture enemy arms by joint action the regular, militia and guerilla forces must split these weapons up among themselves in a fair and reasonable manner.

Whether our long-term resistance war ends in victory or defeat is the common responsibility of the whole people. But naturally, in military affairs, the regular, militia and guerilla forces must shoulder the bulk of this responsibility.

XVI

ELIMINATING WRONG TENDENCIES

In the above chapters, we have made a preliminary criticism of certain erroneous tendencies concerning the resistance. Now, we think it necessary to outline the four major erroneous tendencies, with a view to unifying the thoughts and actions of our cadres and people in the resistance :

These four tendencies are :

1 — Defeatism, pessimism.

2 — Under-estimation of the enemy.

3 — Tendency to compromise half-way.

4 — Tendency to rely on the mediation of a third country.

What do the defeatists and pessimists advocate? They say : Our people are not well armed, our population is not numerous, our country is small and not rich ; if we fight, we are doomed to failure. It is better to get it over and done with, acknowledge French tutelage and accept an " autonomous " regime ! They also say : France has ground, air and naval forces, she is powerful ; what is the use of resisting her, only to go on suffering ? They even say : Our people have a low standard of education, our country is weak, it is not ready for independence. Tran Van Ty, a puppet belonging to the Le Van Hoach clique,[46] dared to utter the vile words, which merit the everlasting scorn of our people : *"Even if France gives independence to Viet Nam, we shall refuse it . . . "*

All these arguments prove that the pessimists, the national traitors, the defeatists, the capitulationist clique, grossly overestimate the enemy and greatly under-estimate our people's strength.

Though our weapons are not good, we have produced new ones with which to resist the French colonialists ! It is certain that the more we fight, the more better arms will be produced. And if we skilfully apply guerilla and mobile warfare, we can use our rudimentary weapons to seize the enemy's superior ones ; with few arms, we can defeat an enemy with many.

It is true that our country is small and not rich, and that our population is not numerous ; but as we have said in Chapter XI (" Our Difficulties and Those of the French "), the enemy's country is far from ours, his troops come from afar, his forces must be split up to fight in many places. The enemy's internal finances and economy were exhausted after the Second World War ; the dissensions between the

[46] Lê Van Hoach, a dignitary of the Cao-Dai religious sect, was Premier of the short-lived Cochinchinese Autonomous Republic from December 6, 1946, to September 29, 1947. He later became a minister in the Bao-Dai government and took refuge in France in 1955 after President Ngo Dinh Diem came to power in South Viet-Nam.

various French political parties are growing ; the struggle between the workers and the capitalists is fierce. As for us, apart from arms, the political consciousness and the level of organization of our people are higher than before. Our National United Front is firm and expanded. The present world situation is very different from that which followed the 1914-1918 World War. The great movement of democracy and independence, which is constantly growing, constitutes a strong rearguard. We have the necessary conditions for fighting. It is possible for us to wage a long resistance, and our long resistance will certainly be victorious. The tendency to defeatism and pessimism cannot stand analysis.

Of late there has emerged a clique calling itself a "Nationalist United Front". It is headed by Nguyen Hai Than, Nguyen Tuong Tam, Tran Trong Kim and Nguyen Van Sam. This clique claims " independence and unification within the French Union " ; in truth these elements are scheming with the old foxes, the Franco-American colonialists, with the aim of destroying our people's resistance and dividing our ranks. The defeatism of these national traitors is more dangerous than the " servilism " of Truong Dinh Tri, or the politics of " autonomy " or "suicide" of Le Van Hoach.

The opposite of the tendency to defeatism and pessimism is the tendency to under-estimate the enemy. Those who are affected by this tendency grossly over-estimate themselves and greatly under-estimate the enemy. They say : We must avail ourselves of the moment before the enemy can send big troop reinforcements, while he has to divide his forces for the struggle in the African colonies, to throw all our forces into a few decisive battles ; we should not protract the war. In their opinion, a protracted war will create suffering for the people and wear out our forces. The above-mentioned line of underestimating the enemy maintains that we should rapidly attack the enemy to reach a quick decision. This is an adventurous line and represents certain suicide. It has the character of desperation. Those who under-estimate the enemy are afraid of him, of hardship and of the protracted war.

If we follow their line, we will make a premature sacrifice of our forces in some initial forced battles ; once our main forces are decimated, we shall become weakened and will not be able to rise again. At the beginning the enemy forces are stronger than ours ; they are at the peak of their strength. As the enemy concentrates his attack to annihilate us, we must avoid battles unfavourable to us, we must preserve our forces for a long resistance. While fighting, we consolidate our forces and weaken and discourage the enemy. Thus, we wait for the opportunity to launch a counter-offensive to annihilate him. Protracting the war does not wear out our forces, but on the contrary strengthens them day by day, as it weakens the enemy forces. If we are afraid that a long war will make our people unhappy, and advocate throwing in all our forces in a fit of anger to end finally in military defeat and national bondage, what hardships will there be then ?

Fortunately, this tendency to " fight rapidly and decide rapidly " is not widespread in our country, and has not very serious consequences. And those who, when the nation-wide resistance broke out, wanted to stake everything on this policy, have more or less admitted their errors and are willing to give up their " flash in the pan " heroism.

The third tendency to be eliminated is the tendency to compromise half-way in the resistance. Those who are affected by this tendency think that if we prolong the war we shall be doomed to failure ; that if we are going to negotiate with France, the earlier we do so the better, in order to avoid sacrifices by our people and losses to our forces. These people become too quickly depressed in the face of the temporary successes of the enemy. Faced with loss of land, they think of loss of the country. They do not understand the twists and turns in the development of war : the enemy wins victory only to be defeated later on ; we suffer defeat, only to carry the day in the long run.

The aim of our people in this resistance war is to recover independence and unity. If France recognizes the independence and unity of our country within the French Union, we may discuss the re-establishment of peace with her. On the other hand, our people will continue their fight as long as France does not give up her designs to invade our country again, or recognizes only sham independence and unity. We will fight to the last man. We will fight to the last breath. We are determined not to compromise, because to compromise is to surrender. The guns are cocked, they are firing. Their task not being fulfilled, the Vietnamese fighters cannot lay down their arms !

Why should the resistance war not be hard ? While fighting, we must rally all the moral power of the people so that they will work eagerly, endure hardships and participate in the resistance to the end. There are battles which wear out our forces ; but there are battles which enhance them. So we must fight in such a manner as to increase our forces. If we surrender and are conciliatory we shall be disarmed by the French; then who will there be to speak of losses and gains ?

Lastly, there is a category of people, a prey to sickly fear, who grow anxious at the mere thought of a long-term resistance war. They think of a simple measure, hoping rapidly to end the war : they propose to reform the government, to eliminate a number of " red " elements. According to them, this will facilitate negotiations with the French and be favourable for diplomatic relations with other countries.

This category of people think that by removing some people from the government the war will cease immediately. How naïve ! Whether the war ends or not is decided by the evolution of the relation of forces between the two sides, but not by administrative measures. The more we " reform the government ", the more we show our spinelessness and make concessions, the more the French will exert pressure on us. This only serves to sow confusion among the people and leaves them in doubt. Why do people who ask for the above " reform " not suggest replacing the reactionaries, the incapable and wavering elements in the administrative machinery at all levels in order to conduct a stronger resistance ? In truth, they are afraid of a protracted war and do not believe that a long-term resistance can be victorious. That is why they seek to use governmental reform as a present to offer to the French colonialists in begging for an armistice. They do not look forward, but always look back. On the road of the resistance war, they are those who turn their backs on the goal, or march backwards. What a pity !

This does not mean that we brush aside reform of the government. There is no government which is everlasting and unchangeable. But ours is a country with a constitution. Our government is constitutionally set up. If reform is needed, it must be carried out constitutionally. And even if it is reformed, our government must be a constant reflection of the solidarity of the entire people : all sections of the people, democratic parties and patriotic personalities, united within the framework of the National United Front, under the leadership of the Communists. We must bear in mind that neither the Vietnamese revolution as a whole nor this resistance war can be successful without the leadership of the Communists !

The fourth tendency which opposes the long resistance, is the tendency to rely on the mediation of a third country. Those who have the above tendency do not believe in our people's power to resist. They have no confidence in final victory. Which is the third country from which they are begging mediation ? It is a powerful imperialist country. How dangerous ! If they demand the mediation of an imperialist country it will play the role of the clever magistrate in the fable of La Fontaine, ' The Oyster and the Litigants ' ; or it will be the " fight between the stork and the oyster for the benefit of the fisherman " all over again.

There is in France at present a clique seeking to call in the assistance of a third country. This clique tends in the direction of submission to the orders of the Dollar God to sell out France and a part of the French colonies to the U.S. imperialists, so as to have sufficient strength to repress the democratic movement in France and the revolutionary movement in the colonies. We refer to de Gaulle and those around him. Do we follow them ?

There are also people who hope for the intervention of the United Nations Organization. We need only remind them that, with its present organization and spirit, the U.N.O. is unable to sanction its members who have committed misdeeds, and is powerless to defend the San Francisco Charter. The problems of Greece, Indonesia and China have proved that even if the problem of Viet Nam were raised before the U.N.O., it would bring no better results. In the future, if we prolong the resistance war, there may be countries which, in the cause of peace and justice, or because of a situation analogous to ours, or from a sense of rivalry, will raise the question of Viet Nam before the U.N.O. But we should not rely too much on others. We should help ourselves, and then we will be helped by others. If we lack courage, no foreign force can bring us freedom and independence.

In a word, the above tendencies are inimical to a long war of resistance. If we do not resolutely combat them, they will develop and cause damage. These tendencies are [47] expressed in words by some people, or are just in the thoughts of others. There are people who express them in deeds, others are biding their time to try and carry them out later. To win victory, we should act in such a way that there is unity of mind among the entire people in the resistance. Eliminating the above tendencies is an important task of our people.

---

[47] This is another expression of Truong Chinh's (and Red China's) "hard line" view that the sole solution to Viet-Nam's problems is protracted war. There is little evidence that his views have changed fifteen years later.

XVII

MOBILIZING THE ENTIRE PEOPLE

This people's war for freedom and independence is very hard and long. To win victory, the whole people must participate in it, shoulder their responsibilities, be courageous and make sacrifices. Therefore, the entire people must be mobilized.

For more than six months, generally speaking, the people throughout the country have been supporting the government and the army : they enthusiastically enlist, actively join the militia forces, help the engineers, ensure the supplies of the army and provide it with information, willingly pay taxes to the government and diligently tend wounded armymen. The most moving thing of all is that the youth in many villages are urging one another to go to harvest rice to help out the families of armymen. What zeal, what selflessness, what exemplary solidarity and patriotism !

Our compatriots in the rear are worthy of the sacrifices of the heroic fighters at the front.

Nevertheless, is this enough ? Not yet ! What forces there are latent in our people that are not yet fully tapped and not yet made use of in a rational manner ! Is there not *still a lot of deadweight* alongside the flourishing forces that are so abundantly contributing to the cause of the Fatherland ? Are there not *still inert elements* not yet stirred by a driving force to take their part in the struggle ? Many reserves in labour, money and material wealth are not yet mobilized in service of the long resistance war.

All this is true. Many villages, lying a long way from the front, are still deep in their dreams ; they do not know yet what the resistance is, they do not yet understand the resistance. The sound of distant gunfire has not yet stirred them from their slumbers.

There are still many areas where the young people consider the sabotage of roads, the building of earthen barricades, helping the army, as they did forced labour under the imperialist regime ; while working they put their heads together to bungle the job, or even run away !

How much money is lying useless in strong-boxes at the bottom of family chests and is not yet used in production beneficial to the country ! The spirit of mistrust, selfishness and stinginess of those who have it is not yet being strongly attacked ; that is why it lies useless while the Government calls for increased production. There are people who use their money for contraband activities, hoarding and speculation, availing themselves of the fact that the country is in danger to make their fortunes. Their money does more harm than good to the nation.

How many able people still consider that the resistance war is the affair of the government and the army, and maintain the indifferent stand of " doing nothing while your neighbour's house goes up in flames. " There are even trained personnel of various branches who impudently draw their pay from the government to spend days and nights playing mahjong and poker, while on the battle-front our fighters are sacrificing their lives for the Fatherland, and while our workers and peasants are straining every nerve to produce munitions for the army, and tools and food for the entire people. There is not as yet any rigorous law on mobilization to discipline these elements, nor any active propaganda to make them see their failings quickly and rapidly mend their ways.

In a word, our weak political mobilization has not yet aroused the burning patriotism of the whole people. The press only circulates superficially, and is read only by a few people ; only people in the areas where the papers are published really get any benefit from them, and there are still many villages which, since the beginning of the nation-wide resistance, have not received a single paper. The agitation groups and shock propaganda units work hard at delivering speeches, but they generally separate propaganda for the resistance, from help to the people in production and in the struggle against illiteracy ; thus, their propaganda becomes drier and drier every day. Information centres have done much work, but are still very few.

The mobilization of the moral power of the people is not yet continuous and widespread. On the other hand, actions that are harmful to the mobilization of the entire people are not condemned or corrected in time. In some places, whenever our troops arrive, they show themselves arrogant and authoritarian, recruit the people by force for " statutory labour ", and put many exactions upon them. In some localities, the Resistance and Administrative Committee is incompetent and remains inactive : it does not know how to mobilize the people and give explanations ; so it issues orders without thought, thus sowing discontent among the people. In some places, Pooh-Bah elements among our cadres, and sectarians, discard able people and genuine patriots from the resistance. In other places, traitors to the nation have wormed their way into the ranks of the people, using money to bribe or female beauty to beguile government workers in order to get information and to discover the whereabouts of government organs. Worst of all is that in some localities, traitors using the cloak of religion have set up the " Viet Kien " Association (Reconstruction of Viet Nam), with the aim of bringing about the autonomy of the Catholic areas, sowing the tendency to surrender and division among our Catholic compatriots, and calling on them not to pay taxes to the government. They make anti-Viet Minh and anti-communist propaganda, but dare not utter a word against the French. They constantly instigate the people to oppose the government's orders, and sabotage our moral mobilization.

We should urgently eliminate these dangerous seeds. Traitors to the nation, reactionaries, and enemies of the resistance must be immediately eliminated. We should punish those even in the ranks of the resistance who have advocated wrong measures or committed harmful deeds. We should wipe out corruption, backwardness, sectarianism, bureaucracy, arbitrariness and militarism, and apply a progressive policy, in the people's interests. At the same time, we must broaden propaganda work in a methodical manner. We should strive to raise the people's political consciousness, enhance their patriotism and vigilance, and foster their fighting spirit. We should use diverse forms — newspapers, books, music, dances, operettas, plays, photographs, exhibitions, emulation, etc, to enable the people to grasp why we must fight, for what purpose we are fighting, how we will win victory — to help them to see that the resistance war is certainly hard, but that it will certainly be victorious. Only in this way will the people enthusiastically assume their responsibilities in accordance with the slogan " Those who have money will contribute their money to the resistance, those who have strength will contribute their strength, those who have talent will contribute their talent ". Thus, no force will be wasted, no force will stand aside from the struggle, no force will be superfluous. Only in this way will the army and militia forces bravely sacrifice their lives to annihilate the enemy ; when one man falls, ten others will rush forward.

However, if we want all the people to take part in the resistance in every field, verbal political propaganda alone is not enough. We should strive to improve the living conditions of the people, lighten their burdens, reduce land rents, restrict usury, take genuine care of the life of the toiling people and the civil servants, etc. To mobilize financial resources, we should on the one hand levy taxes according to democratic principles, and on the other help the people to a better life. Only in this way will the people be brought to contribute to the resistance budget, support the army and risk their lives to fight against the French aggressors and defend their own vital interests. At the same time, we must consolidate and develop the new democratic regime, so that the people feel strongly that they are citizens of a Democratic Republic, and have inalienable rights. So, the people will be determined to make sacrifices, to defend their sacred freedom and their political power, to struggle against the enemy's attempts to re-impose upon them the yoke of barbarous and brutal bondage.

There are people who suggest abolition of the committee system and appointment of administrative personnel. They do not understand that restriction of democratic rights will have harmful effects on the resistance war.

To improve the living standards of the people, to expand their democratic rights — these are two conditions that must be fulfilled if the entire people are to be politically mobilized, if the whole vital power of our twenty-five million compatriots is to be drawn into the struggle.

Mobilizing the entire people is not a job that can be done from one day to the next, it must be carried out constantly and regularly until complete victory ; brief bursts of activity cannot meet the need. We must, according to the development of hostilities, announce our victories with a view to raising the morale of the people and the army. We must draw the lessons of our defeats to educate the people and army in fighting, in combatting espionage, in seeking information on the enemy's situation, ensuring secrecy, supplying the army, tending the wounded, etc.

Nor is mobilizing the entire people a task for the government alone ; it is a task that must also be carried out by the various political parties and people's organizations. So, to carry out regular, wide-spread and far-reaching mobilization both from above and from below, we must strive to gather the people in patriotic organizations and democratic parties. The development of such people's organizations is a guarantee of the success consistency and depth of the mobilization of the people. For instance, to implement rapidly and to spread far and wide an order issued by the government, the various organizations should mobilize their members to respond to that order, cite the organized people as examples, and thus give a good start to the implementation of the government order concerned.

If we neglect the organization of the people, we cannot mobilize the entire people to support the government and the army, and cannot enable them to take part in the resistance in every field.

In 1918 Lenin wrote : " To wage a real war, we must have a strong and well organized rear." (Let's Set to Work, " Pravda ", March 4, 1919).

These words constitute very precious counsel for us in this long-term reisitance war.

CONCLUSION

The resistance war of our people is a revolutionary war, a just war. It has a popular, all-round and long-term character.

Let us examine history, from the liberation war which expelled the Manchus from our territory until now. This is precisely another great liberation war of our people against the aggressors to recover independence. And in nearly a century of French colonialist bondage, this is the fiercest battle of all to crush the invaders and recover our sovereignty.

This war is a very great but also a very hard one. A great task can never be carried through easily ! Out of so much blood and ruin will spring a new, independent, unified, democratic and prosperous Viet Nam.

Of the three conditions for the victory of the resistance war mentioned in Chapter XII, the *unity of the entire people* must of course be the first one. If the people's front of resistance is broad and firm, even supposing that the movement in France against the " dirty war " and the support of the world democratic forces do not prove strong enough, our resistance war, though certainly prolonged and harder, will sooner or later end in victory. The future belongs to us. Final victory will be ours, provided that *the entire people are united, are self-reliant, and wage a long resistance.*

The long-term resistance war of our people must pass through three stages. That is *a necessity.* In the course of the resistance war, negotiations may take place. *Nevertheless, if we have not yet passed through these three stages we will still not win back true independence and unity.*

The enemy of our people is extremely brutal and dangerous. The French and world reactionaries are seeking to crush us by the most unheard-of means before they themselves are finally crushed by the democratic forces. Our difficulties are still many. The task of every Vietnamese citizen is very heavy. The tasks of the *Lien Viet front, of the Viet Minh and of our organization* are still heavier. Our people and the cadres of our movement must be determined to overcome every difficulty and do their duty. With our far-sighted President Ho Chi Minh at the helm, the ship of Viet Nam, with its heroic crew, will certainly cheat all reefs and weather every storm to reach its splendid harbour.

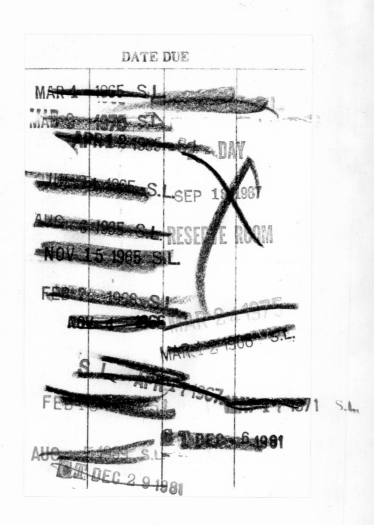